1147454   H 31 350 226-7

HAY, D. 940.545

WAR UNDER THE RED ENSIGN - THE MERCHANT
NAVY, 1939-45   20/10/82   £8.95

Please renew/return this item by the last date shown.

So that your telephone call is charged at local rate,
please call the numbers as set out below:

	From Area codes 01923 or 0208:	From the rest of Herts:
Renewals:	01923 471373	01438 737373
Enquiries:	01923 471333	01438 737333
Minicom:	01923 471599	01438 737599

L32b

Hertfordshire
COUNTY COUNCIL
Community Information

2 4 OCT 2000

1 4 JUN 2001

29 6.01

- 2 APR 2002

- 6 JAN 2003

1 2 JUL 2004

2 4 NOV 2004

- 9 AUG 2010

6/12

L32a

D1460123

THE MERCHANT NAVY 1939-45

WAR UNDER THE
RED ENSIGN

THE MERCHANT NAVY 1939-45
WAR UNDER THE RED ENSIGN

DODDY HAY

JANE'S

First published in 1982 by
Jane's Publishing Company Limited
238 City Road, London EC1V 2PU

ISBN 0 7106 0205 7

Computer typesetting by
Method Limited, Woodford Green, Essex
Printed in Great Britain by
Biddles Limited, Guildford, Surrey

CONTENTS

Photographs follow pages 64 and 128. Maps are on pages 34 and 90.

ACKNOWLEDGEMENTS

To the men and women who have helped me to write this book I must say this is not my story – it is yours. In thanking those who contributed to my knowledge and understanding of the Merchant Navy's wartime role, I express my gratitude equally to those whose individual stories do not appear as to those, or their representatives, whose stories do. Seamen above all others, surely, will need no reminder of the analogy between a book and an iceberg.

There must be those I have met and talked with, in pub or in club, whose names now escape me, and to them I offer my apologies, but the following I have not forgotten and shall not forget. M. Allison, Errington Angus, Roy Bagot, John Bean, Duncan Bennett, Arthur Bird, Jim Bowring, Mrs. Caffery, Sidney Cercell, H. W. Charlton, Rev. E. H. Chevasse, Harry Chivers, C. M. Cooper, John Harding-Dennis, Trevor Davies, L. A. Davies, A. L. Dean, R. J. B. Dunning, Ernest Ellis, W. B. Fenner, R. J. Frinton, Ross Fraser, Rupert Grayson, A. J. Green, George Hindle, Mrs. Frances Hope, Maurice Irvin, John Johnson, Mrs. Mary Lagergren, Johnny Lake, Ron Lang, P. Langley, Cyril Lofthouse, L. B. Lowry, Hughie McNiven and his lady; John William Mahon, R. Marren, Eric Marshall, John McIntyre, Tim McCoy, Amby MacBride, Andrew Moffitt, Henry Norman, Mrs. Sylvia Pearson, Jack Peers, C. D. R. Poole, R. F. Purchase, J. C. Purser, Robert Rigg, Mrs. Mark Simpson, Frank Swinyard, H. J. Thorpe, Mrs. Betty Togneri, Michael Togneri, Roy Trowsdale, A. J. Vinden, Ted Wadsworth, M. C. Ward, E. Whitehead, E. Williams, P. G. Woolcott.

There are, however, certain people and certain institutions to whom especial thanks must be offered for assistance without which the book could not have been written at all. I would mention them now, in no chosen order of priority or importance. Jim Slater, CBE, General Secretary of the National Union of Seamen, himself a survivor of three wartime sinkings and of the Arctic convoys, asked that his own story should be omitted, but made certain, in many ways, that access was available to the men who had served alongside him.

David Jacobs on BBC Television and Malcolm Billings on BBC Radio induced many merchant seamen to write to me about their wartime experiences, as did Douglas Fairey in *Weekend* magazine and Jim Jump in *Seaman*.

Gordon Evans, Director of Square One, was indefatigable in his maritime research and indispensable in his personal encouragement.

Dr. R. Hope, OBE, Director of the Marine Society, very generously allowed me to make use of material already published, to which his Society holds the copyright. Such material was invaluable in reconstructing certain stories.

Phyllis O'Connor of the Marine Society and Patricia O'Driscoll, editor of *Coast & Country* dug painstakingly and invaluably into their records on my behalf.

The librarians of the Imperial War Museum, the Maritime Museum, Greenwich, and the Public Records Office, seemed never to tire of producing relevant books and documents over a period of many months.

At Springbok-Radcliffe Farm, both the residents and the staff appointed by the Merchant Seamen's War Memorial Society accepted me as a friend as night after night I pumped them shamelessly for their wartime reminiscences.

In Russia, researching the epilogue, I met so many helpful men that it is impossible, as in the case of British seamen, to list them all individually. Once again, my gratitude is general, but once again, certain people must be singled out for special mention, because they recreated the world of forty years ago.

Rear Admiral Ivan Papanin, Head of the Maritime Research Department of the USSR Academy of Sciences; Captain Alexander Savelier, who for seven years represented Soviet Merchant Shipping in Great Britain; Orest Sychenikov, President of the Soviet Sea and River Workers Union; Albert I. Goosev, Foreign Relations Officer of the USSR Sea and River Workers' Union; Vladimir Prokoviev, Chairman of the Archangel Regional Committee of the Sea and River Workers' Union; Sergei I. Kuznetsov, President of the Northern Shipping Company; Eugeny V. Segnitov, Chairman of the Murmansk Regional Committee, Sea Workers Union; Vladimir A. Ignativk, President of the Murmansk Shipping Company; Vsevolod Y. Mozhaev, Head of the Foreign Relations Department of the All-Union Central Council of Soviet Trade Unions; Nikolai V. Cherkasov, Head of the West Europe Section of the Foreign Relations Department of the All-Union Central Council of Soviet Trade Unions; Vladimir S. Gordejchik, Assistant Minister at the Ministry of Merchant Marines of the USSR; Vladimir Tikhonov, Deputy Minister of the Merchant Marine of the USSR; Adolf Zagovalko, Manager of the International Seamen's Club of Archangel; Vladimir Lebedenko, International Relations Department of the Murmansk Shipping Company; Valentine Naumenkov and Vladimir Kamenz made magnificent travelling companions over many thousands of miles. Each one of these men made an invaluable contribution to my introduction to Arctic Shipping.

And, finally, my thanks go to my son Iain, who tolerated bursts of enthusiasm and moments of total exhaustion with kindness and with calm, and to my wife Jenny, who had married an airman but remained loyal as ever to a temporary merchant seaman.

Doddy Hay
London: May, 1982

Chapter 1

THE FLEET THAT WENT TO WAR

For its trade, its prosperity, and, in wartime, for its continued existence as an independent nation, Great Britain had for centuries depended upon its commercial shipping no less than upon its naval power. For a variety of reasons, in 1939, the British merchant fleet was in a sorry state. The basic causes of the ailment were the steady advance of overlapping monopolies in all branches of the shipping industry, and the greed for profit of the shipowners. The symptoms were spectacular rewards on the one hand and degrading deprivation on the other.

Almost from the outset of the First World War the major shipowners had become profiteers on the grand scale. The Government had suddenly needed ships of all types and sizes, and the owners had made sure that the Government got them – at inflated rates of hire and at correspondingly high rates of compensation should the vessels fail to reach their destination. When at length, in 1916, a Ministry of Shipping was set up in order to introduce some measure of control, its first Parliamentary Secretary, Sir Leo Chiozza Money, estimated that in the previous two years the shipowners had gained net profits of some three hundred million pounds, and that the capital value of the vessels they owned had risen by a further three hundred million. By the end of that war the insurance compensation paid out by the Government had reached one hundred and four million pounds for the loss of requisitioned ships that had cost originally less than half that amount. In fact, many of those, when first requisitioned, had been worth only a fraction of their listed price through depreciation.

This was an era of coffin ships, rusting, leaking hulks sent out to sea with heavy loads, heavier insurance, and a complement of expendable men. Despite the fast-rising cost of purchase the companies bought more and more vessels, for every ship that put to sea was a guaranteed source of profit, regardless of whether it ever made port. Simple statistics tell the tale. In 1913 the cost of transporting one ton of coal from Cardiff to Port Said was seven shillings; by 1917 it had risen to one hundred and twenty. In the same period the cost of carrying one hundred pounds of cotton from New Orleans to Liverpool soared from thirty one cents to six hundred and twenty-five. As to the insured value of the ships, a 7,500 ton British freighter, valued in 1914 at forty-five thousand five hundred pounds, was rated in 1919 at two hundred and fifty-eight thousand, seven hundred and fifty.

The term shipowners of course includes the shareholders in the companies they controlled, and those reaping the profits were to be found in some strange and disturbing places. On 3 July 1917 the Chancellor of the Exchequer, Bonar Law, made a remarkable statement in the House of Commons. "The sum of money I had invested in shipping, spread over fifteen companies, was £8,100. Five per cent interest on that, which in ordinary times I should be glad to get, would be £405; but for 1915, instead of £405, I received £3,624, and for 1917 I received £3,847. One of the steamers has been either sunk or sold. I do not know. Either way, she has been turned into money for me. In that ship I had £200, and after the very handsome dividend I received, on liquidation I received over £1,000. There is another shipping company in which I invested £350. The other day I received a letter from the Managing Director saying that because of the cost of building ships, they were going to make a division of surplus capital. For that £350 capital, of this division I received a cheque for £1,050."

With the ending of the First World War these vast profits and reserves, plus further Government grants towards repairs and reconstruction, were used by the owners to further and to hasten the drive towards monopoly and to diversify their fiscal interest. The bigger companies began to amalgamate and to swallow up the smaller, and to forge financial links with overlapping interests in banking, mining, wharfage, minerals, aviation, engineering and ship repair, railways, tramways, and tea. The three directors of the Ellerman Lines acquired between them nearly fifty other directorships in associated companies; the thirteen members of the P & O board held over one hundred other directorships in a complex empire of investment and shared control that ranged over Britain, Belgium, and Iberia, China, India and Ceylon, Egypt, South America, Australia and New Zealand. By the time the Second World War was about to break out, five companies and their satellites owned and controlled six million tons of shipping, 35.2 per cent of the British mercantile fleet.

It might be expected that after the hardships and loss of life experienced by British merchant seamen between 1914 and 1919, a respectable portion of this profit and investment would have been set aside for the improvement of their reward and the alleviation of the appalling conditions under which the vast majority of them plied their trade. On the contrary they twice, in 1921 and again in 1925, suffered cuts in wages, the companies putting forward a cynical claim that they were now actually operating at a loss. The sophistry of their argument was insulting; a sop to the stupid, reassurance to those in the know. Cunard, for example, made much in 1920 of the fact that they had reduced the dividend on Ordinary shares from 10% to 7½%. What they neglected to introduce into their plea of poverty was the fact that, in view of a recent bonus issue, the amount of cash they had paid out to the shareholders had *risen* from £148,540 at 10% to £222,810 at 7½%.

As to conditions of life on board ship, the Government paid lip-service to decency by issuing instructions and suggestions regarding space, safety, feeding, and hygiene, but at their strongest these were merely instructions, not laws, and for the most part they were never enforced. The British seaman continued to live underpaid in conditions of filth. No-one would ever have described the redoubtable Lady Astor as a plebeian rabble-rouser, yet this is what she had to say on the subject in the House of Commons as late as 8 July 1938. "There is nothing too strong that can be said in the House about these conditions. It applies to most of our merchant ships today. A medical officer has reported that in some ships the men's quarters are unfit for human habitation. The Government have sent out instructions: but these instructions are not regulations. We are told that the instructions do not apply to old ships. This means that for fifteen to twenty years seamen will have to live in appalling conditions. I got a member of this House to go down to the London Docks and take a look for himself. His comment was that he would not put ferrets into ships where men had to live. That was a very Conservative Member of Parliament."

Another aristocrat, besides Lady Astor, had already made his protest and recorded his observations in an even more practical way. Rupert Grayson, now in his eighties, son of Sir Henry Grayson, shipbuilder, is a man of many parts: successful novelist, King's Messenger, and friend of the famous. Between the Wars he decided to go down to the sea in ships, and not as a rich young man, but in the fo'c's'le, working his passage.

"An old hand named Bill grabbed me by the arm and pushed me for'ard. 'This is where we sleep, mate; and eat, mate.' The fo'c's'le was lined with bunks clamped to the ship's side like double coffins. The air was charged with the reek of stale tobacco and the sour smell of sweating feet; I quickly made my way on deck.

"Breakfast consisted of porridge, in all climates (guaranteed to give prickly heat in the Tropics), on which we sprinkled, very carefully, sugar from our sparse ration. A tin of condensed milk, even when punctured with the smallest holes, was shared with the cockroaches that swarmed in brown-jacketed masses everywhere in the fo'c's'le. The Bosun and the POs, in addition to the porridge, were each given a bloater. The midday meal was usually salted beef or a sinister stew, which was called by the uninviting name of lobscouse. On Fridays we had fish from Iceland, where it had been kept salted on ice for several seasons. This we knew as bacalao, and it required a sharpening of the knives before it could be consumed; to make it more palatable, or to disguise it, the mess was covered with an indescribable sauce known as 'Jessie's Dream.' The puddings were spotted dog and apple waddy.

13

Supper was the left-overs of the Officers' Mess, crouching under a thick spread of dough. The Board of Trade ration of lime juice was issued out of large stone jars as soon as we entered the Tropics. Truly we ate to stay alive, for there could have been no other reason."

Equally graphic was the report of Quartermaster E.F. Agacy that appeared in *Seamen* on 28 September 1938, in relation to conditions aboard a passenger ship carrying first, second, and third class customers. "Mealtimes were occasions requiring careful use of the space allotted to us. Our meals always had to be kept on the deck while two men sat inside their bunks to eat their meals. I had to stand up, and the fourth would sit on one corner of the only stool, resting his plate on his knees. Old tins served the purpose of butter dish and sugar bowl etc. When the ship lurched and rolled we were washed out at times due to a leaking port. We had no place to keep our go-ashore suit and shoes; as a result, our good clothes were always covered in mildew."

On smaller ocean-going ships and on coasters, conditions were often a great deal worse than that. Men working sometimes up to one hundred and ten hours a week in surroundings of squalor, with coaldust, grease, sea water and the cockroach as their constant companions, sought their food and their sleep in semi-darkness under the fo'c's'le head, their iron-frame bunks welded to the steel plates through which the sea at its worst would batter against their ear-drums and bruise their bodies as it threw them from side to side. Those with the will and energy to wash either their clothes or their bodies could make use – in their own time, between shifts – of the zinc bucket issued for this dual purpose. Accommodation for more intimate matters of toilet was a bucket-flushed trough bolted at the entrance to their sleeping and eating quarters. If, coming off watch, they were soaked through, they could try drying their gear, by turns, at the bogey stove in the fo'c's'le that belched soot and smoke at every hiccup. The average wage of the merchant seaman at this time was a little under two pounds ten shillings a week.

From Jim Bowring, who will appear later in this story as a man of authority, a Bosun – comes yet another view of life in the pre-war Mercantile Marine. "My father was a Master Mariner, and he did all he could to put me off the sea. He was determined I'd serve an apprenticeship and get myself a good trade with a pension, but he'd talked too well before that about his own adventures, and though we'd never got on, I'd listened to him, and in 1933, when I was fifteen, I ran away to sea. I became a galley boy, and my pay was one pound sixteen shillings a month – I'll never forget that figure – and when I came home after maybe four months I was rich, with perhaps three quid saved up. No more than that, because I'd squandered a bit, learning about life in foreign ports, but three whole *pounds*, crackling in my pocket, and a wee bit saved over to provision me for the next trip. When that came up I was better off than some of the old hands, who'd blued their lot in the nearest pub and come back on board carrying the Fifty Three Pieces – a pack of cards and a sweat-rag. They were mostly the firemen and the trimmers, and by God, they were a hard lot – well, they had to be.

"Some of them could have broken your back without even looking at you – they were the lucky ones – but there were others that were small, no more than five foot and a bit, and they were the real tough nuts. Well, think of it – they were shovelling coal *above shoulder-level*, opposite their eyes. Looking at these little fellas, you'd think their muscles were going to burst through their skin, and of course they were living like rats – so were we all – and they didn't much like it. I wasn't exactly a softie myself, but I tell you, I wouldn't have tackled some of these boys with a field gun. Funny thing is, there was very seldom any real trouble, and then only when someone had been ashore. I suppose we all realised we were literally in the same boat, and to tell the truth, most of us had never known anything better. It's a hell of a thought, really, but there you are."

A report by the Medical Officer for Hull and Goole summarised in 1938 the conditions of dirty quarters found aboard British and foreign ships under his jurisdiction.

	Ships Inspected	Ships Concerned	Dirty Quarters
British	4,519	105	374
Other Nations	2,360	16	41

Three years previously, in a survey relating not to illness but to industrial mortality as a result of accident, the Board of Trade had issued the following figures, terrible in their significance, but ignored.

Industry	Death Rate Per Thousand
Cotton	.035
Engineering	.095
Ship-building and Repairs	.505
Coal-mining	1.100
Railways	1.730
Seamen	3.040

The overall effect of the living conditions aboard British ships between the wars was less surprising than it was horrifying. In 1938 the Registrar General's Decennial Supplement for England and Wales showed that the death rate for merchant seamen was 47% in excess of the national average, the principal killing factors being tuberculosis, cerebral haemorrhage, and gastric or duodenal ulcers. Six years earlier, and again to no avail, the London School of Hygiene and Tropical Medicine had reported that the mortality rate below the age of fifty-five was twice as high amongst seamen as amongst the rest of the male population.

These were the men, then, upon whom Great Britain called for a life-line during the years of war, and these were the men whose contract ended when the torpedo struck. For the owners had protected their profits to the very end; a seaman's wages ended when his ship went down, no matter where, how, or in what horror.

Chapter 2

EARLY DAYS

If British strategic thinking in 1939 was in many respects still outdated, one vital lesson at least had been learned from the experiences of the past. The island's lifeline, along which would pass troops and material, fuel and food, could be established and maintained by one method and one method alone, the instant adoption of the convoy system for merchant shipping.

The horrendous losses suffered during the First World War before the belated introduction of that system in 1917 despite fierce Admiralty opposition still lived in the minds of Admirals and ship-owners alike, and long before the announcement of war against Germany, contingency plans had already been laid down for the escorting by the Royal Navy of groups of merchantmen along Britain's principal lines of communication.

Within a matter of months – in some cases within days – of the outbreak of war, the system was enforced for coastal traffic between Methil, Oban, Loch Ewe, and the Clyde; Southend, Falmouth, and St. Helen's (I.O.W.), and for ocean-going shipping between the United Kingdom and Halifax, Gibraltar, Kingston and Freetown, Sierra Leone.

What had *not* been grasped by the leaders of the Royal Navy and indeed the Royal Air Force, nor by members of a Government reluctant to spend money upon armament, was the crucial role that air power would play in any future conflict at sea, and for this failure of understanding the men of the Merchant Navy were to pay dearly. At least, however, they were destined to sail in convoy, and for that mercy they no doubt were grateful.

In other respects, too, the merchant fleet during this initial period was being swiftly prepared for its wartime duties and conditions of service. Many of the great passenger liners were earmarked for trooping; others, like the *Rawalpindi*, were converted to the role of Armed Merchant Cruiser, in most cases retaining the majority of their officers and mercantile crew on a voluntary Emergency agreement. Smaller ships were simply being provided, as supplies became available, with some form of defensive armament. If in many cases this armament was pathetic in its inadequacy – a single .303 rifle or a Lewis gun to defend a ship and its company against attack by aircraft or submarines, it must be remembered that this was the seaborne equivalent of the Local Defence Volunteers, fore-runners of the Home Guard, who were training with broom handles and preparing to stave off a German invasion with shot guns, pitchforks, and pikes.

Any man, and especially any seaman, who may have been tempted to doubt the reality of total war for the second time within a mere twenty years, did not have long to wait for a savage awakening to the truth, for within twelve hours of Chamberlain's declaration, the war at sea had begun, a German U-boat commander, Oberleutnant Fritz-Julius Lemp, taking upon himself an instant decision over which his predecessors and their rulers in the First World War had lingered and hesitated for two full years.

The SS *Athenia*, 13,581 tons, had sailed from Liverpool at four p.m. on the day before war broke out, carrying civilian passengers, including many Americans, bound for the United States. Chamberlain's announcement was read to them after they had left the ship's Service on the Sunday morning. Dinner was served at six o'clock, and by late evening the *Athenia* had reached 56° 44'N, 14.05 W two hundred and fifty miles North-west of Ireland – but so had Oberleutnant Lemp's submarine.

With a fine disregard both for humanity and for the rules of war, the U-boat commander immediately and without warning unleashed a torpedo at very close range. John Coullie of Chicago, who with his wife Bella was travelling home on the *Athenia* after a holiday in Scotland, describes the scene of the sinking.

"We were both reading when the torpedo struck. Bella was thrown into my arms as all the lights went out and we were in complete darkness. We went up to the top deck, and what a terrible scene that was – people lying all over the deck, women screaming, children crying, the crew keeping other people from rushing the lifeboats, everything smashed to bits. I went down again to fetch our lifebelts, and the stairs were jammed tight. But I had four matches, and I lit them and let the people get clear, and I was soon back beside Bella. I saw the submarine come up about a quarter of a mile off.

"A boat came alongside and I yelled to them to take us off. A fire-hose was over the side, and a man in the lifeboat got hold of it and told us to slide down. Bella was almost there when a wave washed the boat aside and jerked the hose out of the man's hands; she fell between the boat and the ship, and I thought she'd be crushed to bits. I yelled to her to hang on and I just jumped. I tried and tried to boost her into the boat, but oil was flowing from a burst fuel tank, and everything was so slippery I knew I had to do something else.

"I got one leg over the side of the boat, and I grabbed Bella's foot; another man got hold of her lifebelt, and we somehow got her in, with all of us covered with oil, dirty black stuff that tasted so awful we got sick. Nine hours later we were picked up by the yacht *Southern Cross*."

Others aboard the *Athenia* were less fortunate. Eighteen of her crew and one hundred and ten of her civilian passengers were either killed in the explosion or drowned in its aftermath. As for Lemp, no disciplinary action was taken against him by his superiors, who within months were overtly condoning, indeed demanding, unrestricted war on shipping, including neutral shipping in disputed waters. He went on to gain a considerable reputation in the Fatherland, to be promoted to the rank of Korvetten-kapitan, and to sink another fifteen Allied ships, including the battleship HMS *Barham*, 31,100 tons, off the Egyptian coast on 25 November 1941. Like most of the submarine commanders, however, he did not survive the war, and died in battle when commanding the U-110.

It may be appropriate here to take a closer look at the nature of the U-boat crews and their commanders, who together were to prove the greatest scourge to Allied shipping in the years to come and to constitute, in the words of Winston Churchill, the most dangerous single threat to the Allied cause. It was inevitable that they should be especially hated and depicted in British propaganda both during the war and subsequently, as treacherous, cold-blooded murderers, fanatical Nazis to a man, who preyed upon the innocent, stole up in silence and safety, killed without pity, and crept away secure in their invisibility. They were the natural choice as the villains of the war at sea.

In one respect this view was valid. These were the only men – apart, of course, from Allied submariners – who put to sea for the sole purpose of destroying merchant shipping. Except during training and on patrol, they did not live, as other sailors do, upon their craft, which perhaps significantly were always known to them not as 'ships', but as 'boats'. As to the boats themselves, they and the living conditions aboard them both reflected this sombre circumstance.

The U-boats of the Second World War were pressurised tubes crammed with machinery, men, and lethal weapons. There were no cabins, no compartments even, to separate officers from ratings, engineers at work from their sleeping quarters. Everywhere was a tangle of pipes and cables, folding bunks and folding tables that served both for eating and for the study of charts, and, crowding everything else into relative insignificance, the torpedoes. Up to fourteen of them, grease-covered and weighing one and a half tons each, to be stored in the tubes, and share quarters with the crew fore and aft. There were hammocks slung for the off-duty watch, and between these hammocks hung clusters of smoked hams and sausages, nets full of loaves; the galley was a two-burner stove; for a crew that might number fifty there was one toilet, and that could not be used at depths below eighty feet. There were banks of batteries to provide the power, and the whole boat was soon pervaded with the stench of diesel oil and stale humanity. Every meal, every message, had to be carried by men crouching and creeping their way past working or sleeping companions. It was in these conditions that the men of the U-boats put to sea on patrols that might last for weeks.

As to what manner of men they were, in every respect but one, the wartime categorisation of them as simple killers has been proved wanting. Certainly there were fanatical National Socialists among them, though there were many others who were not, but it was not just politics that sent such men to war under the sea. With the exception of some of the bosuns and engineers, they were incredibly young – the greatest of the U-boat captains, men like Kretschmer, Prien, Schepke, and Andrass, were still in their twenties – and what fired them to acts of immense personal courage and, eventually, of self-sacrifice, was as much eagerness for adventure and an intense pride in the traditions of the German Navy as National Socialism. Their closest counterparts in the early days of the war were, in fact, the young pilots of RAF Fighter Command.

None of this is said in order to glorify them, nor to belittle or excuse the terrible hardships inflicted upon their victims, but simply to reiterate the basic truth that men who fight wars are rarely the men who have brought them about, and that no fighting Service can exist and prosper without good qualities as well as a tragic purpose. Assuredly there were acts of unwonted brutality carried out by individual U-boat captains and the men under their command, but, as will be told by some of the British seamen whose wartime experiences form the burthen of this book, there were also acts of gallantry and compassion. And as to hazard, the proportionate loss of life in the U-boat service, in which only ten thousand survived out of the forty thousand who sailed, was the most terrible by far in the history of naval warfare. They were ruthless, the men of the U-boats, but they were brave.

Such, then, was the enemy. To meet their menace Britain was, in the meantime, calling some strange contenders to the colours. The old *Royals*, *Queens*, and *Eagles* for more than a century had been carrying trippers from London and Liverpool on day-excursions to Southend or, more adventurously, to Ostend or Boulogne. These veterans, some of them paddle-wheelers, were quickly caught up in the more serious business of war, and their achievements, far from being a seaside postcard joke, were as impressive as those of any battleship, and were soon to result in the saving of many thousands of lives. Even before war had been declared, eight of these old steamers had been used to evacuate nearly twenty thousand schoolchildren from the threat of aerial bombardment on London.

It was some months later, however, when the unrelieved pattern of military disaster in Europe and in Scandinavia had brought Britain to the brink of defeat, that these ships of the General Steam Navigation Company and the New Medway Steam Packet Company really achieved greatness. Holland and Belgium had been over-run, Anglo-French military intervention in Norway was turning into a fiasco; and the British Expeditionary Force in France was in headlong retreat. Shipping in British coastal waters would soon be under attack not only from aircraft, but from shore-based batteries of heavy artillery.

Then in May 1940 came the fighting prelude and then the rescue and evacuation of the BEF from the beaches of Dunkirk, and the holiday steamers were in the forefront of both. By the middle of that month the German armoured columns were sweeping everything before them, and the fate of the entire British army in France and Belgium, trapped in a triangle based on the coastal towns of Gravelines and Zeebrugge, hung for several days on the last-ditch resistance of the troops in two ports, Calais and Boulogne. To maintain their desperate grip on these two strategic points, and so to hold up the German advance and allow the surrounded armies a brief breathing space, the garrisons needed urgent reinforcements and, by courtesy of the tripper ships, they got them. On 19 May the *Queen of the Channel*, aptly named, brought the Irish Guards to Boulogne, and on the following day the *Royal Daffodil* took the 2nd Battalion of the 60th Rifles to Calais. Each came back to England crammed to the gunwales with nurses and wounded, and the troops they had disembarked held off the German attack long enough, though only just, for their comrades to be saved in the miraculous rescue operation that followed.

The part played in that epic adventure by these conscripted ships was astonishing, though their commanders' reports upon the action were characteristically laconic. Between 27 May and 4 June, under constant bombardment from the land and from the air, they to-ed and fro-ed between England and the beaches as if tethered by elastic, and they voluntarily moored themselves, often for hours at a stretch, in the areas of greatest danger. Crews ate at their posts, snatched sleep in short respites when they could.

One excerpt from a report by the master of the *Royal Sovereign* gives an indication of how he and his crew passed the eight days and eight nights of the evacuation. It refers to the 29 May, when, after surviving a particularly heavy attack by dive-bombers off La Panne, he had come across the motor vessel *Bullfinch*, crowded with troops, which had gone aground. The *Sovereign*, needless to say, had gone to her assistance. The report reads: "18.15 hours. Bullfinch afloat and proceeded. Commenced embarking troops from beaches. May 30th, 04.10 hours. Hove up and proceeded lower down the beach. 04.30 hours. Embarking more troops. 05.30 hours. Vessel full and proceeded to Margate. 11.35 hours. Alongside Margate pier disembarking troops. 13.00 hours. Left Margate. 18.20 hours. Anchored off Dunkirk, commenced embarking troops."

Each of her sister ships had a similar story to tell. *The Royal Daffodil* brought home no less than 8,500 soldiers, including eighteen hundred on one nightmare, dangerously overloaded trip, from Dunkirk to Dover. The master of the *Queen of Thanet*, informed by the captain of the crippled mail steamer *Prague* that he had two thousand troops aboard, answered unhesitatingly "I'll take the lot", which he did, dropping them safely home in Margate. The *Medway Queen*, a little paddle steamer, made no less than seven return journeys, and saved four thousand men in the process. Between them, all told, the holiday steamers of these two companies rescued thirty thousand men. And all this work of rescue was carried out while the town and the harbour of Dunkirk were ablaze day and night, and the civilians of the Merchant Navy were under fire no less than were the uniformed fighting men they were risking their lives to save. The tripper ships had met their moment of glory, and they had come through the long ordeal with honour and with pride.

Chapter 3

THE BATTLE OF TYNE DOCK

When war broke out the *Santa Clara Valley* (4,665 tons) was butting her way through the Bay of Biscay. A few days later she made a solo voyage, unarmed, to pick up a cargo of Swedish iron ore from Narvik, the port in North West Norway that is kept open all the year round by the warm waters of the Gulf Stream. After this hazardous operation it was decreed that she should be fitted with defensive armament, and that was when her adventures began. Jim Bowring, now safely ashore full of seamanship and experience, was then her Bosun, and he pulls happily on his pint and recalls what happened next.

"At Furness in Sunderland we were fitted with two guns, a 4-inch and a 12-pounder, at the stern. They were proper antiques from some former war, and so was the chap who came aboard to take charge and to teach us how to use them. He was a very decent, convivial sort of fellow, a senior NCO of the Royal Marines brought out of retirement, and he loved these guns like children. He cleaned them and he polished them all the way to Newcastle, where we tied up at Tyne Dock in South Shields.

"We stayed there quite a while, and I was ashore one day, minding my own business in a dockside pub, when I heard a great commotion going on outside. I went out to see what it was all about, and found dozens of people milling around my own ship, including two enormous military police and, being led away between them, my friend the Marine, who had obviously been passing the time the same way as I had myself and was laughing his head off. Then one of my pals from another ship came running up to me, and I'll never forget the huge grin on his face and the words that came roaring out of him: 'Jesus Christ, Bosun, you'd better come quick, and make up your mind whose side you're on – the *Santa Clara Valley* has just declared war on the United Kingdom.'"

The jovial Sergeant had, it would appear, been celebrating a trifle over-zealously, and on his return to the ship the sight of his beloved armament gleaming neglected on the deck had proved a greater temptation than he could resist. He had loaded up the 12-pounder – happily, with a practice round - and he had remembered his old skills in relation to the firing mechanism. On just one vital facet of gunnery technique, however, he had temporarily lost his touch, and he had slammed that twelve pound shell clean through the radio cabin of a startled merchantman moored on the far side of the quay, a piece of inspired marksmanship that has been recalled with reverence in the Merchant Navy, ever since, as the Battle of Tyne Dock.

Under her skipper Captain Donald Lennie of Tobermory, the *Santa Clara Valley* went on to see stalwart service in many oceans until, on 23 April 1941, she lay anchored with other Allied ships, in the clear blue waters of Nauplia Bay, off the coast of Greece. She had come there from Alexandria, where she had been extensively re-fitted to carry a very unusual, living cargo. Her decks and her holds now sported stalls, bins, and drains, troughs for eating and troughs for drinking - the logistic requirements of some two hundred and fifty horses and mules destined for warfare in the mountains and valleys of the ill-fated Greek campaign.

The fact that Allied ships were there at all is sad testimony to the fact that men in wartime are ever at the mercy of their own political leaders, in this case Winston Churchill. During the preceding weeks, the man on the spot, Admiral Cunningham, and other senior naval advisers, had repeatedly warned that to divert military effort and maritime resources to a campaign in Greece was to invite massive losses of both men and material in view of the Royal Navy's inability to protect the convoys from the enemy's over-whelming superiority in air power. This inability stemmed in itself from a political decision, or indecision, that had years before, in 1928, denied to the Royal Navy the introduction of a tachymetric system that measured the course and the speed of an attacking aircraft and fed them into the gunnery control machinery, and had so made naval defences hopelessly inadequate against the dive bombers that repeatedly engaged them. By the outbreak of war this gunnery computer had been installed in the warships of Germany and of the United States - but not in those of Britain.

It had also been impressed upon the Prime Minister that the army in North Africa was within sight of the capture of Tripoli. These port facilities were now supplying Rommel's Afrika Korps which had landed in Tunisia in March 1941 to bolster the fast fading Italians, and to divert some 58,000 Allied troops from this objective would be an act of doubtful judgement. It was speedily and tragically shown to be in fact, something more than that, a disastrous mistake that achieved absolutely nothing and that, in the opinion of military historians, delayed the clearing of the Germans from North Africa by some two years. With Churchill's mind closed firmly against any troubling memories of the Dardanelles, he had dispatched his Foreign Minister, Eden, to Cairo to explain why his decisions were right and would be implemented, and the Allies entered Greece.

By the time the *Santa Clara Valley* had anchored in Nauplia Bay they were on their way out again. Three days earlier the gallant Greeks had capitulated to Field Marshal List's 12th Army which had so quickly sliced through their country. An invasion had turned into a rout, and the ships that had arrived to supply the troops were now hoping to rescue them and take them to the next area of 'conquest', Crete, where a similar fate awaited them at the hands of the German paratroops. It was in the midst of this monumental miscalculation that the *Santa Clara Valley* met her fate. Jim Bowring, the Bosun, recalls the day.

"It was just after eight o'clock on a bright morning, and we were lying a couple of miles off shore. I was standing by the 12-pounder, taking a general look around through a new pair of binoculars I had bought a few weeks before, when I spotted a flight of aircraft coming fast on to us off the land. I counted eighteen, and that was the last cool and competent thing I did for quite a while.

"There was this awful screaming noise as they dived, and we watched the bombs dropping away from them. Next minute I was flat on my face, hugging the gun platform – we couldn't fire on them, of course, hadn't got the elevation – my new glasses smashed, and all hell breaking loose all over the ship. With that very first strike we were on fire and sinking fast by the bow. The animals were mad with fright, and I've never admired men more in my life than the two I watched go to work then, cool as cucumber. One was a captain of the Royal Horse Artillery, and the other was the farrier – Shoey, we always called him. Well, these two drew their pistols, calm as you please, and ran around putting the poor beasts out of their misery; they even went below on the same errand, and that's a very brave thing to do on a sinking ship.

"As for me, I went over the side, and it was a hell of a long dive, for I was right aft, and by this time the stern was a long way out of the water. I couldn't swim, and while I was floundering around I saw something I'm almost ashamed to tell you about. There was another ship quite close to us, the *Cavallo*, and as soon as we were hit she lowered her boats. Well, there was our whole crew in the water, and of course we reckoned they meant to pick us up – but would you believe it? These sods hauled straight for the shore as fast as their arms would pull them – and they hadn't even been hit. Me, I remembered something Shoey had said to me about a situation like this; "if we get sunk, Bosun, trust the horses, but watch out for their hooves or they'll kick you to pieces." Well, there was one right next to me, swimming his heart out, so I grabbed him by the tail – at full arm's length, of course – and d'you know, that beauty towed me straight in to the beach. I hope he found a good home."

Chapter 4

THE SHARPSHOOTERS: 1940

It was uncommon enough for men of the Merchant Navy to receive the major honours and decorations awarded by a grateful nation to their counterparts in the fighting Services. For two such awards to be made following one relatively small incident, and for the same award to be received by the ship's captain and by one of his deckhands, was not so much uncommon as astonishing – but then so was the incident.

On 1 August 1940, the SS *Highlander*, 1,216 tons, steaming 55° 56′ 02° 04′W off the north-east coast of Scotland, was attacked by a flight of Heinkel bombers, diving on her out of a watery evening sun. The master, Captain W. Gifford, ordered a swift change of course, and the crew rushed to action stations, but the *Highlander*, with her puny armament, must have looked to the German airmen like a defenceless, sitting duck. They were soon to learn differently, and to give their lives in the learning.

In his summing-up of what followed, Captain Gifford is characteristically terse. "It was a grand evening's work. Apart from the aerial torpedoes they straffed us, of course, and several of the men were wounded, but we were lucky, especially young Anderson, who did well. One bullet dented his steel helmet, and another grazed the skin clean off his upper lip."

George Anderson of Leith, who was manning the *Highlander*'s Lewis gun, did well indeed, and his brief account of the action speaks volumes for both his resolution and his marksmanship. As the leading Heinkel swooped down over the ship, guns blazing, "I let go with everything I had. Suddenly the black shape of the machine seemed to fill the sights, and I kept pumping lead into it as fast as I could swing the gun. It lurched in the sky about thirty feet away, and we had to dodge to escape it as it fell. One wing caught on the side of the bridge, tearing away some of the railings and smashing the lifeboat. The other wing fell over the deck where we were standing. There was a terrific din, but above it we could hear the cries of the German crew. Then the body of the machine broke away, burst into flames, and fell into the sea – they never had a chance."

The excitement of the day, though, was not yet over. By Anderson's elbow was his friend Laurie Halcrow from Shetland, and Halcrow was thirsting for action. Just six weeks previously his brother had been lost at sea, and as another bomber came diving to the attack he saw it only as an opportunity for revenge. Pulling his shipmate roughly aside, he shouted "Let me have a go, George – I've got something to settle", and he grabbed the handles of the gun.

"It was running in with an aerial torpedo, and its guns were spraying the deck. I let it come closer and closer, and then I really let them have it. I must have scored a direct hit, for all at once it sort of swung over and dived straight into the sea, I thought 'right'."

Laurie Halcrow's gunnery gave him not only vengeance for his brother, but earned him an official commendation. As for George Anderson of Leith, he, like Captain Gifford, was awarded the O.B.E., whose ribbon must have stood strangely in the fo'c's'le of the SS *Highlander*, 1,216 tons.

Chapter 5

"THE HAPPY TIME"

In the autumn of 1940 the war on all fronts was going desperately badly for the British now fighting on alone. France, Belgium, Holland, Denmark and Norway had been occupied, and Italy had entered the war during the last stages of the fall of France and opened a new front in Africa. RAF Fighter Command had been subjected to punishing attacks although it was still fighting and intact. London was under siege from the air, and in September, the first month of the Blitz, had endured seventeen thousand casualties in raids by the bombers of the Luftwaffe. The German armies were massing by the Channel ports with a fleet of ships and barges at their disposal, and the people of Britain waited daily for the ringing of the church bells that would signal the start of the island's invasion.

Against this immediate threat the Admiralty had mustered a defensive fleet to protect Britain's shores, a thousand or more ships of all types and sizes, one-third of which at any given time were on active patrol in coastal waters. Many of these vessels had of necessity been withdrawn from duties in the North Atlantic and the Western Approaches, and as a result the convoys crossing between Britain and Halifax or Cape Breton had even less protection along the route than they had had throughout the first year of the war. Their escorts were more sparsely spread, and so was the force of cruisers and destroyers that went out to meet them during the final stages of each voyage.

The effect of this reduction on Britain's merchant shipping was disastrous and from July U-boats were using France's Biscay coast ports. In the four months from June 1940 losses mounted steadily and alarmingly until, in the month of September alone, U-boats accounted for no less than fifty-nine ships with a total tonnage of 295,335, most of them as they rounded the 'Bloody Foreland', the north coast of Ireland. This was the nadir of Britain's fortunes, the moment when even Winston Churchill feared the war would be lost. This was the first period that the U-boat captains and their crews referred to gleefully as the 'happy time'.

This grisly euphoria stemmed not merely from the rate of almost unchallenged success, but also from the introduction of tactics new to submarine warfare, the co-ordinated deployment of numbers of U-boats in groups known by the Germans as *Rudeltaktik*, pack tactics, and swiftly dubbed with the blood-chilling title of 'wolf-packs' by those on the receiving end. This new development was the long-nurtured brainchild of Germany's submarine commander, Admiral Karl Dönitz, who had been studying, practising, and evolving underwater warfare techniques ever since his years as a spectacularly successful U-boat commander during the First World War. Now, at the age of only forty-eight, he combined maximum authority with the keen and active brain of a professional sailor in his prime, a circumstance of enormous importance, for it prompted Dönitz, arguably the greatest tactical and strategic submariner of all time, to retain *direct* control of the forces at his disposal, even down to the issuing, on occasion, of orders to individual captains on patrol.

The essence of the wolf-pack technique was this. Groups of U-boats would be sent to patrol a specific area, where by use of short-wave radio they were able to maintain mutual contact and, usually, with their main base at Lorient on the French coast, where Dönitz had moved his HQ from Wilhelmshaven in August 1940. The whole method of operation was disturbingly simple – disturbingly, that is, from the British point of view. When a U-boat commander came upon a convoy he would signal to base, shadow the target vessels, and report periodically upon their numbers, their speed, their heading and their escorting forces. Unless a particularly enticing victim presented herself – a tanker, for example, momentarily exposed to attack without risk – he would continue to track the convoy while his headquarters notified and directed such other U-boats as might be in the vicinity. Only when the pack had gathered would the attack be launched, and the effect upon the merchantmen could be devastating. In September they made two such sorties. In the first they sank five merchant vessels; in the second they sank eleven out of a convoy of fifteen.

Another convoy to suffer a concentrated onslaught was *SC 7*, a motley collection of slow-moving ships homeward bound out of Sydney, Cape Breton on 5 October 1940. The speed planned for the voyage was a crawling seven knots and the vessel from which the Commodore, Vice-Admiral Lachlan Mackinnon flew his pennant was the twenty-six year old *Assyrian*, at 2,962 tons one of the smallest ships in the convoy, if not quite the most unusual.

That distinction was shared by three remarkable vessels that had been designed, not for the North Atlantic in winter, but for cruising the Great Lakes of North America. They were strange-looking craft, long and slender, with a funnel standing aft and a towering bridge set high above the bow, and it seemed impossible that they could weather the seas and storms that must lie ahead of them on their Atlantic journey to take up duties carrying coal around the English coast. The rest of the convoy, and doubtless their own crews, gazed at them not only with interest, but with foreboding. In the event, the fortunes of these three adventurers were to prove decidedly mixed. One, the *Winona*, was forced to turn back to Cape Breton with a faulty dynamo on the very first night; another, the *Trevisa*, survived ten days at sea before being blown out of the water by *U-124* under the command of Kapitanleutnant Wilhelm Schultz; while the third, the *Eaglescliffe Hall*, after losing touch with the convoy in mid-voyage, not only made the shores of Scotland alone and unaided, but picked up *en route* twenty-five survivors from the torpedoed Greek freighter *Aenos*, no mean achievement for a vessel more used to navigating the narrow waterways that link the placid Great Lakes.

Despite heavy weather in which not only the *Eaglescliffe Hall* but also two Greek freighters failed to keep station, the convoy as a whole sailed on steadily and uneventfully until 16 October, when they heard the distress calls from the sinking *Trevina*. Against this sad signal they had the heartening sight of the 1,000 ton sloop HMS *Scarborough*, which until then had been their solitary escort, being joined by her sister ship the *Fowey* and by the *Bluebell*, a corvette. These two had been accompanying an outward-bound convoy of the 9,000 ton New Zealand ship *Hurunui*, which had been torpedoed two days previously. The *SC 7* was now only four days from home.

They were spotted just before midnight on the 17th, when Kapitan-leutnant Heinrich Bleichrodt in *U-48* tucked himself in behind them and passed the news of their presence to his headquarters in Lorient before settling in to stalk them. Because of the irregular zig-zagging and sweeping of the escort vessels, Bleichrodt had to contain his impatience for hours on end until at last, when he was resigning himself to the unlikelihood of making an attack before daylight, he found a gap in the defensive screen and fired off three torpedoes. Two of them found their marks. First to founder was the 10,000 ton *Languedoc*, a French tanker now sailing under the Red Ensign, and seconds later the Vice-Commodore's ship, the *Scoresby*, took the second charge amidships. In each case, fortunately, the crews were able to take to the boats.

Bluebell lingered to pick up the survivors while *Scarborough* and *Fowey*, the two little sloops, set out to hunt the U-boat. *Fowey*, a few hours later, broke off to rejoin the convoy, but *Scarborough* continued the pursuit all through that day and the following night, dropping depth-charges whenever she made asdic contact. She did not sink the *U-48*, but she effectively prevented her from tracking the convoy, and so gained for the remaining merchantmen an all too brief breathing-space.

During the evening of the 17th, by pure ill-chance, convoy *SC 7* was sighted by Kapitanleutnant Heinrich Liebe, patrolling in *U-38*. Liebe's brief attack, never pressed home, succeeded only in crippling though not sinking one vessel, the *Carsbreck*, but his sighting enabled him to furnish Lorient with an up-to-date report, and twenty-four hours later, east of Rockall, the convoy sailed unsuspecting into a trap. Lying there in wait for them were five of

Germany's newest, biggest ocean-going submarines, commanded by five of her most daring and experienced captains; Endrass in *U-46*, Schepke in *U-100*, Frauenheim in *U-101*, Mohle in *U-123* and, most feared and famous of them all, the twenty-eight year old Otto Kretschmer in *U-99*, already credited with the sinking of no less than twenty Allied vessels.

Endrass was first to fire, sinking the Swedish ship *Convallaria*, and moments later the *Beatus* from Cardiff went down, followed soon after by the Dutch vessel *Boekolo*. Next the *Shekatika*, a 5,458 ton steamer loaded with pit-props, and then, sinking on the instant and taking all her thirty-four hands with her, the ore-carrier *Creekirk* (3,917 tons). The wolf-pack picked off its targets like ducks in a shooting-gallery, from the tiny Swedish steamer *Gunborg* to the biggest British ship in the convoy, the 6,055 ton *Empire Miniver*, an old American-built trader that had started life as the *West Cobalt* before being sold for war service. Nine ships went down in this initial onslaught, and not a single U-boat was destroyed. Aboard the cockleshell corvette *Bluebell* alone, there were one hundred and fifty survivors of several nationalities plucked from the sea.

As yet the Commodore's ship, *Assyrian*, had not come under direct attack, but she was not to remain out of the fray for very long. Her Second Engineer, Bill Venables, gives a graphic description of her part in the action. "The torpedoes found ship after ship, and each sank according to its cargo; the ammunition ship blew up, the tanker blazed, the ore-carrier sank like a stone. From the bridge Captain Kearon and Admiral Mackinnon saw the periscope of a submarine ahead of us, and asked for all possible speed for an attempt to ram her. I spoke to the three firemen in the stokehold, and they grinned at the thought of the old Assyrian ramming a U-boat. They fired her boilers as they had never been fired before; even with both engines full out her steam was on the feather. It was a great effort. I'm sorry to say all three were killed shortly after."

For nearly an hour the *Assyrian* hounded the U-boat, so close on her tail that she dared not try to turn away, but their speeds were perfectly matched and at last, when a cloud suddenly covered the moon, the submarine seized her chance and slipped away to one side. Admiral Mackinnon, cursing his luck, contented himself for the moment by ordering the release of smoke-floats in the hope of providing at least some measure of protection for the remaining ships under his command. To no avail; the U-boats roamed at will, and the ships were picked off one by one. The off-duty men on the *Assyrian* sipped hot tea and awaited their turn; it came at midnight.

Again in the words of Second Engineer Bill Venables. "When I came on deck I found that the twelve-to-four firemen had already gone towards the fiddley. I went after them to warn them about smoky fires. I was just stepping into the port fiddley when a torpedo struck near the stokehold on the starboard side, right opposite me. I was flung heavily to the deck. The three firemen in the stokehold were killed instantly. Some of the men standing on the boat-deck beside the starboard lifeboat were blown into the sea. I ran to the engine-room; the ship was in total darkness, and I had lost my torch. Everything was deathly still, and there was a strong smell of steam. As I called out to find if the Fourth Engineer was safe I slipped on the ladder and fell into oily water that had risen many feet above the cylinder tops, and I realised I must have lain unconscious on the deck for many minutes.

"Hearing shouts, I went to the fiddley top and found Captain Kearon trying to lift up the grating. The three firemen who had been going below when the torpedo struck had been startled by the explosion and had climbed too high up the stokehold ladder. The fiddley lamp had been smashed, and they couldn't see. Feeling the grating above them, they thought they were trapped, but as I knew which was the loose part of the grating, we soon released them."

There were now only about a dozen men left aboard the sinking *Assyrian*, including the Captain, the Commodore, and three of his staff. And Venables, who still had not lost his powers of observation. "While we were launching the small rafts another torpedoed ship drifted across our bow. She swung away and as if in self-sacrifice stood on end. Her bow reared vertically above the sea and she whined as she slid below the water. She carried thousands of pit-props, and these burst from her holds as she sank. Those of us still on the Assyrian were now in a sorry plight. We had neither boat nor raft. The ship's bow was submerged and she was listing to port. The water made a mournful sound that turned one's stomach as it soughed up and down the alleyways. Later I heard a voice calling me from the fiddley; it was one of the trimmers, and it was now more than an hour since the torpedo had hit us. We got him out, but he was terribly injured; his legs were almost off and his stomach was torn open. One of us stayed with him most of the time, wrapping him in blankets, giving him water, and trying to make him comfortable. We could do no more."

Those few men still on the ship, from Captain and Commodore down to seamen, knew very well that time was running out for them, and they found their several answers. A raft they had tried to construct from pit-props started to break up even as they pushed it overboard, but it served for a time to support, amongst others, Admiral MacKinnon and Captain Kearon. Others cut the falls on a damaged lifeboat, and when it floated on the water upside down, they crouched on its keel. Bill Venables settled for a couple of pit-props that he tucked under his armpits as a float and he swam around for several hours, determined to live in this vast loneliness, singing to himself and fighting off the icy grip that was creeping from his stomach up, as he felt, towards his heart. After two hours a submarine passed by within yards of him, but he went unnoticed; after two more he saw the dark silhouette of the sloop Leith, and lost consciousness as he was hauled aboard, to revive only after he had been assiduously massaged for sixty minutes by his rescuers. There were other survivors from his ship already aboard the *Leith*, though

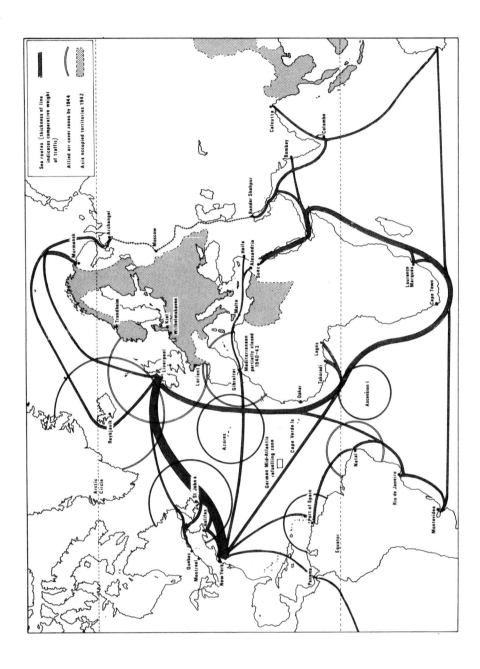

two of them died later from exposure. Amongst those who did *not* die was the incredibly tough Scottish Admiral, Lachlan MacKinnon, who, like the youthful Bill Venables, had supported himself with balks of timber and who had defied both the bitter waters of the Atlantic and his own fifty-seven years.

But the wastage, the loss of brave men, was appalling. The *SC 7*, in one dreadful night, had lost sixteen ships; with those that had gone before, she had lost twenty, more than half of the number sent out from Cape Breton just two weeks before. This was the Merchant Navy in 1940. This was the opening phase of what came to be known as the Battle of the Atlantic.

Opposite: Great Britain's trade routes 1939-45

Chapter 6

THE TENBY GUNNER: 1941

Norman Haskell Thomas was born in 1921, in the Pembrokeshire town of Tenby. His father was a hairdresser, his grandfather had three times been mayor of the town. This is how he is remembered, sixty years later, by his sister, Mrs Sylvia Pearson:

"As a youngster Norman was a bit of a tearaway. Once he shaved off all his eyebrows before going to school; the teacher was concerned because he looked so awful, and asked him if he felt ill. Norman said yes, and was sent home, but he was soon back there, because my mother spotted what had happened. Another time he was hit behind the ear with a cricket ball, and he spent all that night with a pillow over his head so that mother wouldn't hear him crying – but it was a hospital case, and he went through a mastoid operation without a whimper, under local anaesthetic.

"He joined the P&O liners *Strathallan*, *Strathaire*, and *Molltan*, first as a bell boy and later an attendant in the Smoking Room. On one leave he'd spent all his money, so he took a job as a driver, delivering the Christmas post; he'd never had a driving lesson in his life. Didn't bother him a bit, and he never hurt anybody.

"The mastoid operation stopped him from joining the Royal Navy, which he'd set his heart on, and when war broke out he became a gunner in the Merchant Navy. The last time I saw him he was going back to join his ship, the *Gaithsoppa*, and I remember him saying it all seemed so senseless. But before he left we went to visit some friends, and his vocal rendering of "The Storm", accompanying himself on the piano, had us all nearly in hysterics – he couldn't play a note.

"Sometimes it seems a life that was just thrown away and forgotten, without anyone caring."

One may question whether any life given as Norman Thomas gave his was "thrown away", and he was not forgotten, not quite. One man, besides his family and friends, did care, and doubtless still remembers. The following passage, taken from the local newspaper, the *Tenby Observer* of March 28th

1941, was contributed by the sole survivor of the *Gaithsoppa*, her Second Officer, and it tells how Norman Haskell Thomas spent his last and arguably his finest hours.

"Immediately we were torpedoed in mid-Atlantic on February 16th, everyone rushed to collect papers, food etc. I got away in a boat with thirteen others, under heavy machine-gun fire from the submarine. The rudder was broken; there were no oars. The compass was four points out. We had twelve biscuits each, and no water. The biscuits were too dry – we did not want them.

"With our first bearings we headed for Nova Scotia. Having been used to sleeping in the daytime in India, we decided to sleep as much as possible by day and be guided by the stars at night. The Gunner complained of sore feet, took his boots and stockings off, and threw them overboard. He never complained again. Second day out two shipmates were buried. Next day another burial. The following day two more were lowered into the sea.

"The Gunner was going back and fore trying to keep everyone cheerful. We all kept a look-out for passing boats, but there were none to be seen. Buried three more next day. Two more two days later. Now only four left. Still no sign of help.

"Now very, very cold. The Gunner and myself still pretty good under the circumstances. An Indian seaman and the Wireless Operator not so good. Friday night the Gunner and myself prayed fervently for sight of land.

"Saturday March 1st, land ahead. Buried Wireless Operator. Now only three left. Indian boy nearly beat. The Gunner and myself still have fight left, but feel weak. Got to the Lizard. Indian died.

"Took off shorts, hoisted them on pole. Lighted flares. Boat dashed on rocks by heavy seas. Both thrown out. Next I distinctly remember asking 'Am I dead?'. Felt it was pleasant to die – altogether different from what I'd imagined it to be. They lifted me up to convince me I was still alive.

"They tell me in hospital I kept on calling Gunner Thomas. Not surprised, as during these twelve not very pleasant days I had become fond of the lad. Never do I expect to meet with greater courage and fortitude in one who was no more than a boy. They told me he was dashed on the rocks and drowned.

"So, au revoir, my gallant shipmate. Deeply regret you failed to make safe landfall."

A life thrown away, a man forgotten? Surely not.

Chapter 7

THE SINKING OF THE *SPRINGBANK*

In September 1941 Roy Bagot, at the age of nineteen, was very possibly the youngest fully qualified, foreign-going Second Officer in the Merchant Navy. One year later, having been torpedoed off the Canadian coast in the *Dartford*, he suffered so severely from exposure that his career in the Service was over. Today, as President of J.D. Potter Ltd., The Admiralty Chart Agents, he devotes a great deal of his time to helping sailors and ex-sailors in need, and he has never lost his lifelong fascination with the sea. And yet, despite his own ocean-going achievements and experiences, the wartime memory foremost in his mind is of a ship in which he did not serve, the *Springbank*.

"She had just been converted from a freighter to a catapult ship carrying anti-aircraft armament and a Fairey Fulmar aeroplane, and she was making her first voyage as a convoy escort. I was on the coaster *Coxwold*, and we were one of twenty-five vessels homeward bound from Gibraltar in five columns of five. We were carrying damaged aircraft, having thankfully discharged our cargo of high octane aviation petrol for the *Ark Royal*. *Springbank* positioned herself on the starboard quarter, only a few cables away from us, and her mere presence seemed to spread over us like a blanket of authority and protection. Each night, as the sun went down, she would move from her station, passing so close to us we could exchange waves with her crew, and she would tuck herself just astern of the convoy, clear to go into action at a moment's notice. At the time, we seemed secure enough."

Convoy *HG 73* was very far from being secure. Only a few sea-miles to the north, off the coast of Ireland, another convoy, *OG 74,* was under attack by both German and Italian submarines. On 19 September several of them began to converge upon *HG 73*, and on the 20th, the Italian submarine *Tortelli* made contact. *Tortelli* was depth-charged and driven off by HMS *Vimy*, but ahead of them the German *U-201*, having sunk three merchant-men, began moving south to engage the new target. On the 24th *HG 73* was circled by an FW 200 reconnaissance aircraft that stayed prudently out of

39

range of *Springbank*'s defensive fire, and in a desperate gamble the *Springbank*'s captain ordered his single aircraft into the attack. After thirty minutes the Fulmar had made no close contact with the enemy, and was forced to break off with only just enough fuel to see her home to Gibraltar. These catapult launches were once-only missions, and that abortive sortie meant the end of any air cover for Convoy *HG 73*.

With their position and course known to the enemy, the convoy now swung away through ninety degrees, deeper into the Atlantic, but a speed of only seven knots could not possibly carry the vessels to safety, and next day their progress was once again being observed from above. Aboard the Commodore ship, the *Avoceta*, a Liverpool liner carrying one hundred and twenty-eight passengers, most of them women or children, Rear-Admiral Sir Kenelm Creighton received a series of alarming reports; the first stated that two U-boats were already in contact, and those that followed told him that the convoy was being shadowed by no less than a dozen. The reports were accurate, and the *Avoceta* itself, in the event, was the first victim, torpedoed with a great loss of lives on 25 September. For two days the attacks continued and more vessels went down, and as Roy Bagot remembers, on 27 September it was the *Springbank*'s turn.

"At 01.13 hours a ship to port of her was torpedoed, and at once *Springbank* went zig-zagging in search of the attacker. Starshells lit up the whole scene, and from the bridge of *Coxwold* I watched as if it were broad daylight. Two torpedoes hit her as she went in – both on her port side, one aft and one for'ard, and great columns of water and smoke rose up to meet the rain as she rolled away with her wounds. I whistled down to my captain, who came racing to the bridge, and we broke the rules and put about with the intention of following her up. It was wrong, of course, to put our own ship in added danger, and we knew it was wrong – but almost without choice we did it.

"It was blowing gale-force, with a heavy sea running, and we dared not come too close. We tried to come up to windward and drift down, but the gale set her down faster than our own ship moved; we tried to come up slow ahead to her stern, but every time we reduced speed for a safe approach we lost steerage way until our only hope was to lay off down wind, and there we could not stay long, for the screaming wind was blowing *Springbank* down on to us. But we positioned ourselves as best we could, and I signalled our intentions. We rigged ladders and ropes along our port side, and luckily, as we rolled in the troughs, our freeboard was not too great – in fact we were almost up to the gun'ls. There were sailors in boats, sailors on rafts, sailors just swimming, and sadly there were those we watched just drifting away. The crew of the *Coxwold* were all to port, tying bowlines, heaving ropes, trying anything to drag these men aboard, and as soon as one of these fellows was rescued, he would turn right round to lend a hand. It was hellish, but it was inspiring, too.

"We didn't even try to catch up with the convoy; the enemy were still all around us, and with the coming of dawn we would be a sitting duck. With our mission accomplished, and the *Springbank*'s survivors tucked safely in bunks and blankets, we scanned the waters and we zig-zagged our independent way for home. We berthed in the Mersey, and as we walked down the gangplank, close by the Liver building where the ferries come in, there were friends waiting for us beside the canvas screens that sheltered the quay. And do you know, as we came down to greet them, these waiting people, as if they had known what had just taken place, started – very slowly, shyly at first, not all of them knowing the words but each one of them understanding the message – these people started to sing:"

"Eternal Father, strong to save,
Whose arm hath bound the restless wave,
Who bid'st the mighty ocean deep
Its own appointed limits keep;
O hear us when we cry to Thee
For those in peril on the sea."

Chapter 8

TREVOR DAVIES FROM TAFF'S WELL A VETERAN - AT TWENTY

"Taff's Well's in the valleys, you know, so of course I was down the pits when I was fourteen; that was in 1936. But I only weighed seven stone, see, and it wasn't doing me much good, so after three years the doctor said I ought to get some fresh air in my lungs. Well, I sort of fancied Switzerland, but I settled for Cardiff, and it was there I joined my first ship, the *Empire Volunteer*, 5,319 tons, as galley boy. Up till then my idea of the sea was a day out at Barry Island."

Before very long the boy from the valleys, Trevor Davies, was to know a good deal more about the ocean than that. They sailed first for Milford Haven to join a convoy bound for Halifax, Nova Scotia, and "when I saw all these ships moving out together I honest to God thought 'maybe they don't know the way'. I tell you, I was as ignorant as the Graig Mountain." On the outward journey he began to learn his basic trade, helping to prepare and to serve endless meals, to clean out the galley and see there was plenty of coal for the fires, to fix the blackout curtains over the ports as the sun went down, but it was on the long voyage home from Sydney, Cape Breton, with ten thousand tons of iron ore underneath him that his education really began.

"The cook was always hammering at me to wear all my clothes when I went to bed and to take my life-jacket with me, and it was that – and old Cookie himself – that saved me. We were about five hundred miles off the Irish coast, and I'd gone to sleep one night feeling ever so proud and thinking what a story I'd have to tell Mam and my pals back home, for we were the Commodore's ship, leading the whole convoy. Then the whole damn world just fell in on me and I was out of my bunk and horribly awake. The lights had gone, men were shouting and screaming, officers bellowing orders, and I just don't remember how I got to the deck.

"Then suddenly there was Cookie, God bless him, grabbing me by the arm and yelling 'Over the side with you, Trev, and start swimming away; never mind the bloody boats, boy – there's no time.' So I jumped, and the cold

Atlantic hit me like a hammer. But Cookie had been right; she was an ore-carrier, remember, and I learned later she went down in just over a minute.

"The convoy had scattered, and we were on our own, swimming around in the Atlantic five hundred miles from shore, nothing around but darkness and the cries of wounded or drowning men. I heard someone shout 'Try and keep together', but my instincts guided me and I thought no, if I get among that lot I'm finished; someone will panic and grab me and drag me down. So I stayed on the fringe and let no-one come near me, no-one; I don't really know even now if I'm proud of that quick thinking – but I'm still alive, and for that matter still at sea.

"But we'll talk about that later. For five hours on the night of 15th September 1940 I was paddling around in the ocean a long long way from Barry Island. Then, just when I was beginning to feel it was all up with me, the Norwegian ship *Fido* hove to alongside us, and I and the other survivors were hauled aboard her and taken to Belfast. I left that city with trousers, shirt, a pair of slippers and a coat, and I arrived back in Taff's Well with a different story from the one I'd been rehearsing during my last night on the *Empire Volunteer*, and a lot more knowledge than I'd had when I left."

On his next ship, the *Newport*, the excitement for Trevor Davies was confined to being in Montevideo on the fateful day when Kapitan Langsdorff made his terrible twin decisions, to scuttle the Graf Spee, Germany's most powerful warship and to take his own life in expiation of the self-imposed disgrace. But after the *Newport*, Davies was to make another voyage, and then another, of tragedy and personal adventure.

He was by now an Ordinary Seaman, and with his closest friend, Charlie, he joined the *Hazelside*, 5,297 tons, in Cardiff, scheduled to join another convoy from Milford Haven, this time bound for the Middle East with a cargo of Army requirements, including tanks, lorries, and amphibious vehicles that were lashed on deck. That cargo was to seal the ship's fate.

"Everything was all right until we arrived off Freetown for bunkering, but then the weather turned foul on us, and we were in real danger of losing the vital deck cargo. With two other slow ships, the *Nalsie Manor* and the *White Crest*, we were ordered to leave the convoy, and told that the three of us would be given a destroyer as an independent escort. Again everything was fine – for two days. Then the *Nalsie Manor* was sunk, the destroyer turned back to pick up survivors and take them back to Freetown, the *White Crest* just disappeared, and we were on our own.

"I was on watch one lovely night, two hundred miles south-west of Wolfe's Bay, and at one o'clock the Second Mate told me to fetch up some coffee and to bring the lookout aft from the fo'c's'le head. Well I fetched the coffee, and I fetched the lookout – and then it happened. A torpedo struck us forward of the fore-mast, and the bow just disappeared. The lookout man dropped his coffee – and his jaw. 'My God' he said softly, 'I was standing there sixty seconds ago.'

"At least, this time, we had a minute or two to spare, and we put the boats in the water and pulled away, while the *Hazelside* just slipped quietly under. When daylight came we took stock, and things didn't look too bad; we had twenty three men aboard, two tanks of water, and what looked like adequate provisions. But we didn't realise what lay ahead of us, and what followed was a succession of disasters, a living nightmare.

"It started with the boats: the heat had opened the seams of the strakes, and for the first day or so it was all baling. Then the sea got up, so it was out with the sea-anchor and ride it out, and with six inches of freeboard and twenty three men, it wasn't all that easy. But finally the weather cleared and it was time for cleaning, up sail, and head for Africa, two hundred miles away. The wind was good, the sails were full, and for two days we felt great; the seams had hardened, and we were on our way home.

"Then all at once things changed. We found that one of the tanks was contaminated with sea water, and suddenly we were on short commons - one thimble of water a day, and half a biscuit. We had cans of corned beef - but try taking that down a dry throat. Half at a time the crew would go overboard to cool off and to just moisten their lips with salt water, but it was hopeless. Then we spotted a log covered in barnacles. I'm a good swimmer, and I went over the side, swam out and retrieved it, while the rest of the boys kept an eye out for sharks - for days we sucked barnacles and were glad of them. We were in a pretty bad way, our bodies all covered in blisters and our feet swollen out of all recognition. We had no water at all: sometimes we would see a shower of rain and we would row towards it just as hard as we could, but we never reached one in time. We had a hand-operated radio, but it was waterlogged and useless.

"On the eighth day one of the Maltese firemen went berserk. He had been drinking sea water, and after a while he died, so we put him over the side, and I think one or two of us half-envied him. And then, around the tenth day, *we spotted the albatross.* I said 'Lads, there's a bloody good meal', and gradually the idea caught on. We coaxed that bird, we *wooed* that bird, with bits of broken biscuit, a titbit, it settled on the water, and then another titbit. Another. Easy, easy. Don't frighten it. Come on, my beauty, another stretch of that lovely neck. Come here, my white darling, wingspan or no you're our bloody dinner. Closer, just a little closer - oh God, I love you.' Everybody silence.

"Well, we got him, but we were weak and he put up a hell of a fight, till at last someone settled it with a chop across that long neck. We drained the blood, and we drank it, and we cut up the meat so that each man had a piece, and it kept us going for a few days longer. That was enough, as it turned out, but it was a very close call. Strong men were looking like skeletons, and on the fourteenth night, when I took my turn at the tiller, I remember the Chief Officer saying 'Davies, if you are a religious man, pray hard this night, for we shall never see tomorrow.' Well I prayed all right - we were all praying

45

anyway – and in the early hours I heard a noise and for a second or two I wondered what could be causing it. Then there was no mistaking that wonderful, blessed beating of an engine. We were yelling and waving like madmen, and then the *Malayan Prince* picked us up and took us to Cape Town."

Davies and his shipmates spent seven weeks in hospital and at last came home in style on the *Viceroy Of India*. There they went their several ways, but he and his friend Charlie decided to stick together, and after a leave with their families they went back to sea in the same ships, first the *Kingborough* and later the *Empire Cromwell*, (5,970 tons), which they joined in Cardiff on 25 May 1942. Again carrying stores for the army in the Middle East, they set off around the Cape of Good Hope and came safely enough to Lorenço Marques where they lay at anchor for twelve weeks, awaiting the arrival of a replacement ballast pump.

They sailed eventually, alone, and travelled safely through the Mozambique Channel, the Red Sea, and Suez to discharge their cargo at Beirut, and the return trip was equally uneventful as they made their way back through the Canal and around the Cape on a heading for Trinidad. Then on the night of 28 November 1942, the peace of the Caribbean was shattered by a horrendous explosion as a torpedo struck straight into the engine room.

"What a shambles. With lifeboats smashed, the engine room flooded, and men everywhere lying dead or wounded, she was going fast. The Chief Engineer's cabin was right above where the torpedo struck, and I looked in to see if I could give a hand, but the man was finished. Already the main deck was under water and two of the rafts had got away safely; that left one – but it was tangled in the rigging. We could feel the ship going under our feet, so we just clung like limpets to the raft and prayed that the suction might drag her clear. It did, but at once we jammed again under the crosstrees, and by now we were under water and drowning. Then for no clear reason the raft broke free and shot to the surface, with seven very frightened men hanging for dear life on to anything they could lay hold of.

"We looked around us and counted heads on the other two rafts; there were twenty-two survivors in all, and of course my first thought was for my mate. I shouted across and asked 'Where's Charlie?' and the answer came in the most terrible words I have heard in all my life, words that haunt me to this day. 'He went back to look for you.' Twenty one men had gone down with the *Cromwell*, but a lot of them were dead before she sank; my pal had been safe, away in one of the rafts, and the only reason he was dead was that he must have *really* looked for me, gone below and been trapped, for otherwise he'd be bobbing around somewhere on the surface in his life-jacket."

Trevor Davies's anguish was at least temporarily overtaken by events, for at that moment, in a swirling wave of foam, the submarine that had sunk them broke surface, and the figure of its captain appeared in the conning tower. The survivors crouched silently, tense, wondering which type of

U-boat captain he was. Would they be machine-gunned in the water? No: a request was made to see the skipper or the Chief Officer. Informed that all the officers had gone down with the ship, the U-boat commander said in good English that he was sorry, and offered, if there were any wounded or injured, to treat them aboard the submarine and return them to their rafts. There were no takers, and the U-boat quietly submerged.

Trevor Davies had now survived his third sinking in the space of two years, and what is more he had, with a fine sense of impartiality, employed each of the only three methods of survival available to him: the life-jacket, the life-boat, and now the raft. It is scarcely surprising that his shipmates were willing to listen to this twenty-year old veteran when he drew on his hard-earned experience. What water ration should they allow? None at all, was his uncompromising advice, not at least for the first few days. For as long as they could they should exist on their body fluids, which certainly would not be available to them after a few days under the tropical sun. Right from the start, he warned, they should prepare themselves mentally and physically for a long wait. They followed his advice, but on this occasion, happily if ironically, such stoicism was not to be called upon for very long.

On the fifth day they thrilled to the sight of an American aircraft circling overhead, and then to the arrival a moment later of a life-jacket parcel dropped within yards of them, a parcel containing fruit juice, cigarettes, and a message reading "This is from the US Army Air Force. You will be picked up sometime this evening. Good luck - see you on the beach." The Americans were as good as their promise, and that night the survivors of the *Empire Cromwell* were picked up by two MTBs and taken to Trinidad, where for two weeks they were handsomely looked after before being shipped back to the U.K.

Trevor Davies, who later went on to become the youngest bosun in the Booth Line of Liverpool, is a thoughtful man, as well he might be, and he now says "When the end came in 1945 I was an A.B. aboard the *Merchant Royal*, and when we docked and I went ashore, and I saw all this hilarity and singing in the streets, I just stopped dead. I thought of men I'd seen scalded and screaming, mates you could not help, stuck in a port-hole, and many other things, and I thought 'You buggers, you just don't know - and worse than that, you just don't care'."

Chapter 9

THE ARMED MERCHANT CRUISERS

Some sixty passenger liners were taken over by the Admiralty in 1939 for conversion into Armed Merchant Cruisers, and two in particular won unforgettable places for themselves in the annals of Naval warfare, the *Rawalpindi* and the *Jervis Bay*.

Each was a sizeable civilian ship assigned to wartime duties for which it was fundamentally unsuited and inadequately equipped. Each was commanded by an officer of the Royal Navy but manned largely by a crew who had, days previously, been merchant seamen untrained in the arts of war, each went to its death gallantly and unflinchingly in the face of odds that were not only impossible, but were seen to be so by every man from the very outset of the action. In November 1939, in Scapa Flow, the *Jervis Bay* sustained damage to her windlass and had to go to Tyneside for repairs instead of taking up her duties, as planned, on the Northern Patrol. Her place was taken by the *Rawalpindi*, under the command of Captain Edward Kennedy, RN, father of a son Ludovic who has since achieved distinction in other fields of endeavour.

And so it was the *Rawalpindi* instead of the *Jervis Bay* that was cruising between Iceland and the Faroes on the afternoon of 23 November 1939, just fifty days after the outbreak of war, when she found herself borne down upon by one of the most formidable enemy vessels afloat, the German battleship *Scharnhorst*, mounting nine 11-inch and twelve 5.9-inch guns, with a top speed of close on thirty knots. In speed, in range, and in hitting power the *Rawalpindi* with her eight 6-inch guns, cast in the 19th century, was totally out-classed. The *Scharnhorst*, as she closed to within three miles and turned on to a parallel course, chivalrously signalled an order to heave to.

Captain Kennedy's immediate response was to turn sharply to port and to make for a bank of fog, and when it became obvious that he would never reach it before being overtaken he next swerved to starboard and headed towards a large pack of floating ice. The *Scharnhorst*, effortlessly keeping pace with him, fired a single shell across the *Rawalpindi*'s bows and once again sent a signal to heave to. If logic and expediency carried any weight under such circumstances, that order might justifiably have been complied with, for at that moment another vessel came within range – her range – on the *Rawalpindi*'s starboard beam; it was the *Scharnhorst*'s sister-ship, the *Gneisenau*, and the fate of the British ship and her crew now rested solely upon her captain's decision. He was given every opportunity to consider it, for now from the *Scharnhorst* he received no less than three separate orders to abandon his ship. The first two such orders Kennedy ignored; at the third, he opened fire. One shell hit the *Gneisenau* amidships; a salvo directed at the *Scharnhorst* fell short of its target. Now all that remained was time.

Both the *Scharnhorst* and the *Gneisenau* opened up with their heavy guns. The first salvo from the *Scharnhorst* wiped out most of the men on the bridge; the *Gneisenau* kept pace by killing every man in the *Rawalpindi*'s fire-control centre and a good many of her gunners, who were rapidly replaced by anyone free and able to lend a hand; next, an exploding shell wrecked the engine-room and put the ammunition-hoist out of action, and others set the crippled ship ablaze from stem to stern. Yet still the *Rawalpindi* did her dying best to hit back, even the walking wounded helping to manhandle the shells to those guns that were still in action. Captain Kennedy, making his way aft to set up a smokescreen as some tiny measure of protection, was killed alongside the two sailors he had detailed to help him, but for a further forty-five minutes the British ship continued to return the enemy's fire until a salvo from the *Scharnhorst* landed in the main magazine and blew the *Rawalpindi* apart. Two hundred and forty of her officers and men died with her, and only a few survived – but their account of the fight she had put up was blazoned across the pages of the newspapers, and worked wonders for home front morale. As the Prime Minister said in the House of Commons four days later "Their example will be an inspiration to those who come after them." In the time of Captain Bligh and the *Bounty*, much the same thing was said about the cat.

The damage to the windlass of the *Jervis Bay* earned for the ship a reprieve lasting almost exactly one year before she too met her end. This came on 5 November 1940, when she was sole escort to thirty-seven merchant vessels, Convoy *HX 84* bound for Britain out of Halifax. The *Jervis Bay*, although at fourteen thousand tons some two thousand tons lighter than the *Rawalpindi*, carried similar armament, and for six months had sailed under the command of Captain Edward Stephen Fogarty Fegen, RN, a muscular, taciturn, forty-eight year old bachelor wedded only to the Service and a man of almost frightening personal courage.

Fogarty Fegen, along with one hundred and eighty nine of the men under his command, gave his life in the action of 5 November, and earned the Victoria Cross in the giving. It is certainly true, too, that the self sacrifice of the *Jervis Bay* in launching a single-handed attack upon the German battle cruiser *Admiral Scheer* played a vital part in the saving of all but five of the merchant vessels that comprised Convoy *HX 84*, and was thus of greater value than the self-inflicted loss of the *Rawalpindi*, although the actions of the two captains were undoubtedly based upon the same fundamental belief, that the commander of an armed vessel simply does not surrender his ship.

Late in the morning of 5 November the convoy, now half-way across the Atlantic and a thousand miles from home, was overtaken by a five and a half thousand ton banana boat, the *Mopan*, that was making her way unescorted to England, and it was this vessel, not the *Jervis Bay*, that was first to encounter the *Admiral Scheer*. It was this encounter, and the almost incredible reaction to it of the German cruiser's commander, Captain Theodor Krancke, that did more than anything else to save the convoy.

The *Admiral Scheer*'s spotter aircraft had already reported the presence of a major convoy ahead, and Krancke was speeding to the attack, determined to go into action during the hours of daylight, when he came upon the *Mopan* by pure chance. Of all the options open to him he elected the most timorous and the most time-wasting. Ordering the *Mopan*'s captain to maintain radio silence, he also gave orders that her crew should make themselves his prisoners, and he waited a full hour while her seamen pulled their way towards him in rowing boats, before finally sinking this unimportant target by gunfire. Whatever may have been the true motive of the *Mopan*'s captain in obeying Krancke's instructions, by so doing he gained precious time without which Fogarty Fegen's courageous action would have been in vain, and the survivors of *HX 84* may count themselves blessed that they did not come face to face with an adversary of greater wit and resolution. For Krancke's hesitation did more for them than gain time; the smoke from the sinking *Mopan* was seen by the convoy's lookouts, and Fegen was put on full alert for the subsequent attack.

When the *Admiral Scheer* at last came into view the time was nearly five o'clock on a winter's evening, and the light was failing fast. The *Jervis Bay* immediately steamed ahead to challenge, and aboard the *Cornish City* the Commodore gave the order for the convoy to prepare to scatter. At a range of eight miles the German ship opened up with her 11-inch guns in a broadside that set the *Jervis Bay* immediately on fire, yet for twenty minutes more she pressed in, closing the range and keeping the enemy's heavy armament fully engaged. In the process she was subjected to great damage, and her casualties were enormous; Fogarty Fegen himself had one arm blown clean away, yet continued to direct the action until another shell-burst killed him. One remaining gun was still firing defiantly as the *Jervis Bay* went down, having at the end attracted not only the *Admiral Scheer*'s long-range guns, but her secondary and light armament as well. Before then the cruiser had managed to inflict a certain amount of damage amongst the merchantmen, five of which were lost, but as night fell the rest of the convoy disappeared under the safe cover of darkness, and sheer selfless courage had served in the end to avert what would otherwise have been a massacre.

Chapter 10

GENTLEMEN ON PAROLE: 1940

It is agreeable, when engaged in a discussion about modern warfare, to hear the term "parole" used advisedly and without affectation by a man who has given his word, who has honoured it, and who has, perhaps more surprisingly and more significantly, seen it honoured also, in retrospect, by His Lords of the Admiralty. Such a man is Mr. C.D.R. Poole, who in November 1940 was Third Officer aboard the R.M.S. *Rangitane*, (16,712 tons) of the New Zealand Shipping Co., running through Panama to London with passengers, a mixed bag of New Zealand Servicemen and youngsters on their eager way 'home' to join up. On that distinction depended the treatment accorded to those aboard the *Rangitane* when she met her end, intercepted and sunk by two German surface raiders the *Orion* and the *Komet* some three hundred miles east of East Cape, New Zealand. The men on the *Rangitane* were divided neatly, decisively, and honourably by their captors into two groups, players and reserves.

The conduct of both sides in this incident is interesting. The action had been fierce; in the words of 3rd Officer Poole "They caught us in darkness, switched on their searchlights, and opened a murderously accurate fire; with one of them on each beam and their supply ship behind us we were a sitting target, and the attack was savage. We were holed in several places, some below the waterline; the super-structure was riddled and torn, fire broke out all over the ship, and the passenger accommodation suffered worst of all. Five passengers were killed, including three women, and a fair number wounded; two stewardesses and three ship's company were killed too, and a lot more badly hurt. The steering had gone and the ship had stopped. Then they suddenly stopped firing, and took us all aboard as prisoners. They sank the *Rangitane* and we all steamed north – and on December 6-7, with us aboard, they sank five more merchantmen.

"There were six hundred and seventy-five prisoners aboard these three ships, confined below decks for twenty three hours a day, and in the stifling heat this could be pretty appalling. But when our senior officer, Captain

Upton, appealed to the German captain to split our one hour of exercise into two thirty minute periods, so that our quarters might be aired during the heat of the day, he immediately, instead, gave us an extra half-hour for this purpose. Again, he listened quietly to Captain Upton's argument that the young men on their way to join the RNZAF were not as yet combatants, and with scrupulous fairness agreed that they should be put ashore as free men at the first port of call. Next, to our astonishment and delight, we sailors learned that if individually we would give our parole, promising to take no further part in hostilities against Germany, we too would be released – a throw-back, almost, to the days of chivalry. The captives aboard the *Orion* were not so fortunate; her commander, equally within his rights, released no-one, and they all ended up prisoners in Germany."

After re-fuelling at the Marshall Islands, it was the German commander's intention to put his captives ashore on Naru Island, but when bad weather prevented this he set course westwards for the Bismarck Archipelago, where, on 20 December, Poole and his companions were set down on the Pacific island of Emirau. Once again the scene presents a sense of theatrical unreality. After a glass of whisky the German commander offered his hand: "Goodbye, Captain Upton. In putting you all ashore I have kept my word of honour; I am sure you and your men will do no less." Of this Mr Poole now says; "I know that all the officers did honour their parole, and I have no reason to believe differently of any of the men."

Poole continues: "The island was about ten miles long, and occupied by about two hundred Kanakas. The copra production was managed by two Australians. The three ships were flying the Swastika fore and aft, and they first sent a landing party ashore, armed with cutlasses and pistols, to take possession of the island in the name of the Third Reich. The two Australians agreed to this with cheerful realism, assuring them that the provision of food for an extra five hundred guests would raise no problem – an abundance of tropical fruit could be easily supplemented by fish and wild boar there for the taking. We were ferried ashore in relays to begin a week's holiday in this island paradise, the Germans replenished their dwindling larder with fresh fruit and fresh meat, and the conquest of Emirau passed off like a well-organised Christmas party.

"Christmas itself, well, that was an unforgettable experience. We decided to hold a midnight service on Christmas Eve around a makeshift altar on the jetty, and it was strange – and very moving – to find ourselves, as the moment approached, winding our way in single file through the coconut palms, hurricane lamps held high, and singing all the best-loved carols including, of course, Silent Night."

"A couple of days previously, having commandeered the island's small motor-schooner, a party of officers had set course for Kebiang, eighty miles away, to inform the authorities of the situation, and on Christmas Day a flying-boat of the Royal Australian Air Force touched down in the lagoon with supplies of food, cigarettes, and other requisites of a really marvellous celebration. It brought the news, too, that within forty-eight hours a ship would arrive to pick us up and return us to freedom and civilisation. That night we lit huge fires on the beach and ate mountains of barbecued pig and the goodies delivered by the flying-boat – truly, a memorable Christmas, and a reminder now that even in these dark days, on both sides, certain standards of human conduct could and did prevail."

Chapter 11

SINBAD

"We were running alone from New York to Panama, when the lookouts reported what might have been a submarine decoy, and we went to Action Stations. But it was no decoy; it was a raft, flying an old rag from an oar wedged upright, and there was a man lying on it. I took the Accident Boat away while the ship steamed round in circles, about two cables off, and as we closed the raft I could see it had been in the water a long time, from the weed that showed on its underside when it lifted with the swell.

"The man aboard it, burnt black with the sun, was in a very bad way, and he could manage only one word, over and over again – 'bastards'. 'He's a Paki, sir' said one of the crew, in explanation presumably of both his colouring and his limited vocabulary, but he wasn't; he was a 'white' American seaman, the only survivor of four who had dragged themselves aboard the raft after their ship had been torpedoed. The submarine's crew had then turned their machine-guns on them, and this lad had the bullet scars on mind and body to prove it. Hence the 'bastards'.

"With careful nursing, and never being left alone for one moment, day or night, he eventually recovered, and only then would he let me open a package tied securely round his neck. In it there was a card with his name, his brother's name and address, and a handful of dollars 'to pay the cost of passing on the news of his death.' The card was dated thirty days before we picked him up. We called him Sinbad, and he told us quietly one evening that if we hadn't arrived when we did, he had already made up his mind to slip over the side that night. He had no water at all, for it hadn't rained, and though he had a couple of Horlicks tablets his throat was so swollen he couldn't manage to force them down. He'd resisted the temptation to drink sea-water, thank God, and so his brain was all right. We put him ashore eventually at Colon, and the whole crew lined the rail and cheered Sinbad as he hobbled down the gangplank on his crutches. A great lad – I wish I could remember his name."

This story is told by Captain R.J.B. Dunning, who in 1942, when it took place, was Chief Officer aboard the *Hororata*. An ex-Conway cadet, he was already a sailor of great experience, having served as Chief on many ships since as far back as 1933. Of his wartime service he says as if apologising for failure "I never got my feet wet", yet reading his record one can only marvel at his luck, for throughout the war he sailed the Atlantic and other oceans like a commuter. And like a commuter he knew his rights, and how to secure a corner seat.

In May 1939 he had been appointed to stand by as Chief Officer of M.V. *Suffolk*, then building at John Brown's Shipyard, Clydebank, and in September of that year he suffered the first vicissitudes of war. "They came and painted her grey – and between you and me, I'd been very friendly with the Chief Painter and the Foreman Rigger, if you know what I mean, and well . . . between us we'd managed to wangle a few things and have her all beautifully done up in the Company's colours."

There were other indignities to follow. A 4.7-in gun was fitted on top of the deck house, and two Royal Marines were added to the ship's company. "They formed two gun crews and drilled them every day, and as Heads of Departments, trying to work up new ship and a new crew, we were *disgusted*." Reality set in later, and as Captain Dunning cheerfully acknowledges, he and the other heads of departments had cause to be grateful for that 1917 vintage gun and for the Royal Marines who understood its workings. "On a practice shoot we found the firing-pin didn't match the gun. Well, the senior Marine made a sketch, I had a quiet word with the Chief Engineer, and an old shipmate of mine, good with his hands, made up a new one; it fitted perfectly, and everyone was happy." And so the *Suffolk* went to war.

She sailed first to Cape Town, where she was entrusted with a cargo of bullion amounting to two million pounds in gold bars, to be carried to Australia. Dunning's second bad moment of the war came when two of his young cadets, ordered to carry out an independent check, reported to him that one case was missing. Frenzied investigation proved the precious cargo intact, and he is not sure to this day if he had been the victim of youthful, and one suspects very risky, humour. After this and other voyages between Australia and the U.K., he came ashore to a dock staff appointment while waiting to join the *Hororata* under the same captain as had commanded the *Suffolk*, and a further coincidence was to follow.

"We were on our way home from New Zealand and Australia, sailing alone about seven hundred miles west of Ireland, when despite the misty weather the lookouts spotted a lifeboat and we stopped ship. There were twenty men aboard her, survivors from one of the Union Castle ships, I think the *Rochester Castle*. I was on deck by the rope ladders, directing operations, when the lamptrimmer beside me said 'there's MacIver, Sir, who was with us on the *Suffolk* – a really good bloke.' As he came over the side I stuck out my hand and said 'welcome aboard, Mac.' A great thrill that, to have saved an old shipmate. They had been adrift about fifteen days and were in pretty poor shape; in fact one of them, the Sparks, had died only a few hours previously. We pulled the plug in the boat and let him drift away; the rest of them we landed in Liverpool three days later."

Dunning was now given command of the *Empire Manor*, a new ship fitting out in Sunderland, but a telephone call ordering him immediately to London warned that something even more momentous was afoot. Within hours his wife was on her way to stay with friends, his daughter to boarding school in Maidenhead, and Captain Dunning was en route by air and sea to Malta via Algiers. He arrived to take command of the *Essex*, 11,063 tons, which had been severely damaged by bombing a few months before, and he received orders to report to the Vice Admiral, Malta, on the following afternoon.

"I decided that first of all I'd take a good look at what I was being let in for, and so I borrowed a skiff, pulled out to the *Essex*, and rowed all round her; then I went aboard, and by the time I had carried out a solo tour of inspection I knew that I had a tough job on my hands. She was moored alongside the huge American tanker the *Ohio*, which had been all but sunk on the epic convoy that saved Malta from starvation and surrender, and they were a sad and sorry pair.

"Next day I had my appointment with the Vice Admiral, Sir John Mackenzie, who told me I must take the *Essex* out of harbour immediately to make room for ships scheduled to take part in a major operation, which turned out to be the invasion of Sicily. He was a little startled, to say the least, when I gave him a list of repairs I wanted carried out before I took the Essex anywhere at all, but I stuck to my guns, and next day a great horde of dock workers were swarming all over her and making good her defects. Amongst other things, they had to weld patches over literally thousands of holes in the hull, and to prepare *some* sort of accommodation for myself, officers, and ratings.

"Five days later I had to report to the Vice-Admiral again. After a talk about the ship he said 'I'm glad you're not so bloody miserable as you were a week ago', and I answered 'With respect, Sir John, would you have taken a ship to sea with thousands of holes three feet above the water-line?' He gave me a long look, but all he said was 'Carry on, Dunning.' Within twenty-four hours we'd moved out of Valetta Harbour and anchored between Malta and Gozo. The *Essex* was still little better than a wreck, for she'd been a regular target for bombers for nearly two years. The original attack had caught her fair and square, killing eighteen officers and men, gutting the amidship accommodation, and, worst of all, flooding the engine-room. The intention when I took over was to see her back to U.K. for repair and refitting – but even the Vice-Admiral eventually agreed she had to be made reasonably seaworthy first.

"It was a slow and frustrating business, but at least we had a front seat view of the Sicily show, which was very soon under way, and though we twice dragged our anchor and narrowly missed going aground, we gradually turned her into a ship with some chance at least of reaching our first objective. Algiers. After I had scrounged a couple of lifeboats that had been picked up by a ship off Sicily, and a reasonable supply of food, the officers and twelve seamen of a Boom Defence vessel that had just reached Malta agreed to crew for me in exchange for passage to Algiers. With them and a handful of Maltese sailors, we were ready and waiting when three Naval tugs arrived on 21 August to take us in tow, and we reached Algiers safely on the 27th."

"Here I found both officers and seamen waiting for the ship to turn up, and that was a huge relief, for they were a fine bunch, and several of them had sailed with me before. There was good news, too, for the Boom Vessel boys who had helped out, for it was agreed that they too could make the passage home to England. I had already promised the same to the Maltese, and so everyone was happy. Of course it was no simple matter; two of the Naval tugs saw us to Gibraltar within a couple of days, but there we lay at anchor for twelve weeks before a Dutch tug, the *Zwarte Zee*, arrived to take us in tow for U.K."

It was to be an eventful voyage, and yet again a ship's company had cause to be grateful for Captain Dunning's Conway training and seafaring experience. "The weeks we spent at Gibraltar weren't wasted. We carried on with repairs as best we could, of course, and on one or two trips ashore I got friendly with an officer of the RASC, and told him a sad story. The stove we'd left Malta with was about the size of a gas cooker in a council flat, and I now had a ship's company of thirty five. Well, the lovely man invited me to choose a complete field kitchen; with the help of the Chief Steward and the Cook, both old shipmates of mine, I did just that, and throughout all the troubles and worries ahead, we were never without a hot meal."

On 24 November, towed by the *Zwarte Zee*, the *Essex* finally left Gibraltar and was joined in the Straits by ten other slow ships of different sizes and nationalities, as well as by two other damaged vessels in tow. Next morning came a rude shock. Captain Dunning again: "At daylight, not a sign of the convoy, just the two other cripples and ourselves. Then a Destroyer steamed alongside and informed me that the tows were to sail on alone, escorted by three trawlers. Well my God, we had literally no armament, not even a rifle, but by this time I was past worrying, past caring even. The senior ship was the escort trawler *Blackfly*; I had met her Commander at the Convoy Conference, an RNR officer I felt instinctively was a good man, and I was happy enough to leave the initiative to him."

For a week all went well, but on the 8th day, as they rounded Cape Finisterre, the weather became suddenly wild, and all went violently, unbelievably wrong. By nightfall they were hove to in a Force 8-9 gale, when without warning the tow wire parted; "we were adrift in pitch darkness, and we were rolling about like lunatics in hell."

Morning came at last, but the winds had not abated, and even in daylight

there was no sign of the *Blackfly* the *Zwarte Zee*, or any other of the ships or
tugs. They were still rolling at least thirty degrees each way, and it was with
real thankfulness, two hours after daybreak, that they watched the trusted
Blackfly pull alongside and heard her Commander promise that he would
stand by them all the time until the winds should lessen and the tow could be
reconnected. That relief was not to come until the following day, but for some
hours anxiety was held at bay by the herculean task of repairing the newly-
inflicted damage that was causing them to wallow so desperately out of
control. It was in fact brutally simple to assess – the rudder stock had broken
loose and was hanging only by the lower pintle – and brutally hard to put to
rights – "but at least it kept our minds off other matters."

There were still wickedly high seas running when the *Zwarte Zee*
manoeuvred under the lee bow to make the reconnection, and Captain
Dunning is unstinting in his praise of the Dutch captain's seamanship, which
won the admiration of every man in the *Essex's* crew. "His skill was quite
amazing, and it was with real pleasure, after we'd crept safely to anchor in
Falmouth Bay, 17 days from Gibraltar, and 16 *weeks* from Gozo, that I had
him and the *Blackfly*'s commander aboard to crack a bottle of liqueur whisky
I had been saving especially for the occasion."

There were to be other memorable occasions before it was all over, for
Captain Dunning, later in command of the *Cornwall*, sailed on in convoy
between England, Halifax, and New York until the end of the war, but he
came safely through it all. In August 1946 his experience was put to good use
with the command of the training ship *Durham*, where groups of fifty cadets
were sent to benefit from it. He came ashore in 1950, but even then he had a
further twelve years ahead of him as a Marine Superintendent in Australia
before returning to England and retirement.

Chapter 12

THE ESCORT GROUPS

If there is one man outside the official ranks of the mercantile marine who can claim his place in any story of the Merchant Navy at war, that man is the late Captain F.J. "Johnnie" Walker, CB, DSO and three Bars, RN. Any fighting man who wins the DSO four times in as many years must be regarded as someone out of the ordinary, and Johnnie Walker did this in the service and protection of British merchant seamen. His personal contribution to the increasing safety of the convoys throughout the middle years of the war was immense, so huge and demanding, indeed, that it cost him his life, not as a direct result of enemy action but through sheer weariness and strain self-imposed during his unremitting struggle against the menace of the U-boats. In the early hours of 9 July 1944, at the age of only forty-seven, he died of a cerebral thrombosis; in the words of his medical attendants, "Captain Walker's death is considered to be attributable to the conditions of his Naval Service."

His superior officers in the Royal Navy were more lucid and equally to the point. In the words of Admiral Sir Alexander Madden, KCB, CBE, RN, "Captain Frederic John Walker, RN, was a forthright and practical man, full of faith and action in everything he undertook. He was a high-principled, courageous, modest and kindly naval officer, who looked exactly what he was – an outstanding leader of men." Admiral Sir Max Horton, who commanded the Western Approaches in which Walker found his greatest glory, said "Victory has been won and should be won by such as he. May there never be wanting in this realm a succession of men of like spirit in discipline, imagination, and valour, humble and unafraid. Not dust nor the light weight of stone, but all the sea of the Western Approaches shall be his tomb."

Walker's wartime achievement may be summed up simply; he was both the brain and the sinew of the Royal Navy's Escort Groups, the sloops and corvettes that switched the British role in the battle at sea from the defensive to the attack, and that slowly changed the German U-boats from the hunters into the hunted.

Like many great leaders in all arms of the forces, British men like – Wingate, Farran, Mountbatten, Embry – he was a strange man, a brave idealist with a darker side to his nature, a natural captain of games with a strong and pleasing personality, yet who took a positive delight in killing for what he considered a good cause, and describing his successes in terms best suited to the slaughterhouse, an academic who stamped and cheered out loud on the bridge of his sloop, muffler waving in the wind, like a hearty housemaster willing his adolescents to muddy victory in the under-fifteens' rugger cup. His men worshipped him. To understand why, one need do no more than look at two clauses he included in his instructions to the nine ships under his submarine-hunting command. "It should seldom, if ever, be necessary to conclude a signalled report with the words 'Request Instructions.' and 'No officer will ever be blamed by me for getting on with the job in hand.' But the officers to whom this *carte-blanche* was given had been drilled and trained to the limits of endurance by Walker himself before these instructions were issued. They were trusted individualists, but they were acting every moment as members of a team, with the team's success always as the objective and with Walker, always, as its coach and captain. The toast with which he greeted, in November 1941, the inauguration of his new command "To the 36th Group and the total destruction of the enemy" was typical of the man and of his philosophy. So were his invariable order to "splice the mainbrace" after a kill, his sailing into battle to the tune of "A-hunting We Will Go" blaring out from his ship's loud-speakers, and, perhaps most significantly, the almost unbelievable insensitivity of his recorded remark after a sunken U-boat had yielded up, *inter alia*, a side of bacon and a sailor's lung; "The bacon was well-cured" reported Captain Walker, CB, DSO, "but the lung was very new." He was a church-going man who said prayers with piety over the bodies of his own dead.

Yet, whatever sombre corridors ran through the structure of his personality, Johnnie Walker, within the context of the war, was a Godsend to the men of the Merchant Navy – a ruthless, relentless tactician dedicated to eliminating the men who were hunting them down, in which cause he was brilliantly successful. He dreamed up for Western Approaches Command a technique of saturation depth-charging and maximum illumination that would effectively cut off a submarine's only lines of withdrawal, and he named this operation "Buttercup" in homage to a family pet-name for his wife. He maneouvred the ships under his command as a single entity, and on 17 November, aided by a young naval pilot, Sub-Lieutenant George Fletcher, who lost his life in pressing home the attack, he scored his first success, destroying the *U-131*, a seven hundred and forty ton ocean-going submarine under the command of Korvettenkapitan Arend Baumann, as it stalked the Gibraltar-bound convoy *HG 76*. Just one day later Walker's Group sunk the *U-434*, whose commander, Kapitanleutnant Wolfgang Heyda, brought his boat to the surface under heavy attack in a successful bid to afford his crew

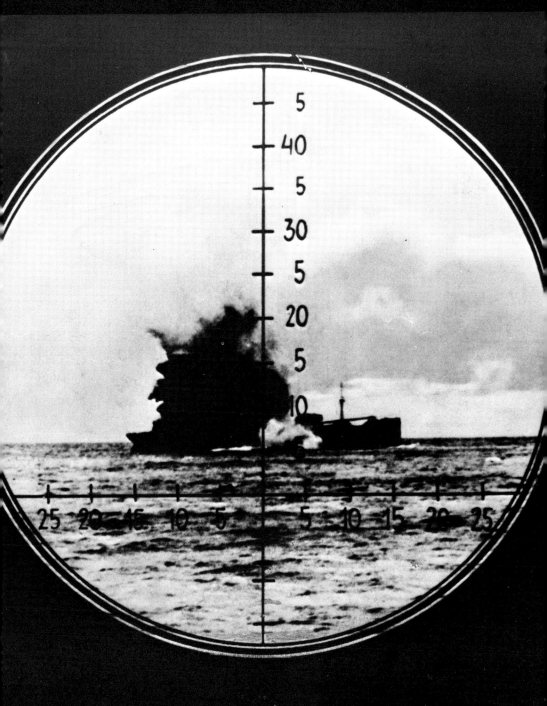

The end of a merchant ship, seen through a U-boat's attack periscope (Ullstein)

A.   MERCHANT NAVY DEFENCE COURSE, PART I.

NAME (in full)	Maurice William Irwin.			
Usual Signature	Mau Irwin.			
Grade and No. of Board of Trade Certificate	2ⁿᵈ MATE.		Year of Birth	1914

Session	Subject	Port	Date	Initials of Instructing Officer
●	Trade Protection			
B	Convoy	SOUTH SHIELDS	4 DEC 1939	
C	Signalling	SOUTH SHIELDS	5 DEC 1939	
D	Defence against Submarines	SOUTH SHIELDS	7 DEC 1939	
E	L.A. Gun Control	SOUTH SHIELDS	6 DEC 1939	
F	L.A. Gun Drill	SOUTH SHIELDS	6 DEC 1939	
G	Air Defence and H.A. Gunnery, Part 1	SOUTH SHIELDS	7 DEC 1939	
●	Defence against Mines	SOUTH SHIELDS	5 DEC 1939	
K	Defence against Gas	SOUTH SHIELDS	4 DEC 1939	

Signature of Instructing Officer on completion of Course.

COMMANDER,
M.N.D.I.O., SOUTH SHIELDS.

17521/9835   5m/7/39   Wt & Sons Ltd   2090c/65547/672

Above: Early days – crew of a U-boat watch for targets – 1940 (Ullstein)

*Left: Early days – Second Mate
Maurice Irvin's completion
certificate for the Merchant
Navy Defence course – all
packed into four days of
December 1939* (Irvin)

*A remarkable photograph of the
Christmas dinner enjoyed in 1940
by the crew of the* Rangitane
landed by the German raider
Komet *on the island of Emirau
in the Bismark Archipelago.*
(C. D. R. Poole)

The crew of a channel steamer pictured in Dover shortly after Dunkirk

MERCHANT NAVY A/A GUNNERY COURSE.

CERTIFICATE OF PROFICIENCY.

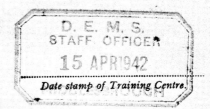

D. E. M. S.
STAFF OFFICER
15 APR 1942

Date stamp of Training Centre.

Name...... M.W. IRVIN.

Rank or Rating...... 2nd Mate.

B. of T. or D.B. No......

has completed the Merchant Navy A/A Gunnery

Course and is qualified in the firing and

cleaning & oiling Marlin Hotchkiss & Lewis

~~maintenance of a~~......

machine gun.

Rank...... COMMANDER, R.N.R.

D.E.M.S. D.E.M.S. STAFF OFFICER,
Training Centre MIDDLESBROUGH.

883 13836/5078 6 30M 5/41 JP 16/70b/1
902 15650/5104 20M 5/41

Left: Stripping the Lewis gun on an armed trawler. Above: Maurice Irvin's DEMS proficiency certificate for Marlin, Hotchkiss and Lewis machine guns (Irvin)

A U-boat finishes off a torpedoed tanker with shell fire (Preussischer Bildarchiv)

Deadly adversaries for the Merchant Navy – a U-boat and a Junkers Ju 88 meet in northern waters
(Ullstein)

The British tanker Gretafield *burns after torpedo attack early in 1940*

DAVIES.

5   **CERTIFICATE**

Or Certified Extract from List
and copy of Report of Character

No.	*Name of ship and official number, and tonnage.†	Date and place of Engagement.*	Discharge.	*Rating.
1	s/s. *newbury*. N.T. 3196. /149773. London	11·10·40 Newport.	6·8·41 London VicDKs.	Deck Boy.
2	Hazelside 16579H Newcastle NRT 3108	11·9·41 Cardiff	28·10·41 Cardiff	O.S.
3		9·...	1 2 APR 1942 SWANSEA	Os
4	s/s "EMPIRE CROMWELL" SUNDERLAND OFF. No. 168920 GROSS 5970.14 NETT 3577.00 N.H.P. 415.	25·4·4. CARDIFF	27 NOV 1942 AT SEA	O.S.
5	s.s. Fort Ash Prov. Reg.	15·3·43 Cardiff	26/6/43 Dock St.	Sailor E.D.H
6	Barrgrove 142279	1 3 JUL 1943 CARDIFF	14/11/43 Barry	Sailor.

* These columns are to be filled in at time of engagement.

Deck boy's progress — pages from Trevor Davies' continuous certificate of discharge charting his career from eighteen-year-old deck boy (already the veteran of a sinking) to the end of 1943. Hazelside and Empire Cromwell were both sunk by U-boat attack

DAVIES.

OF DISCHARGE 6

of Crew and Official Log Book,
if desired by the Seaman.

Description of voyage.	Copy of Report of Character.		Signature of (1) Master; and of (2) officer and official sta...
	For ability.	For general conduct.	
1 Foreign	VERY B 73 GOOD	VERY B 73 GOOD	(1) EXTRACTED FROM ~~THE OF CREW &~~ (2) Dip Hahuggan for REGISTRAR GENERAL 17 December 1959
2 Foreign	VERY 212 GOOD	VERY 212 GOOD	(1) As per O.L. 1942 (2)
3 Foreign	VERY B 93 GOOD	VERY B 93 GOOD	(1) Irma Lwd (2) G. I. James SWANSEA 8 APR 1942
4	VERY B 154 GOOD	VERY B 154 GOOD	(1) (2) DOCK STREET
5 do	VERY B 118 GOOD	VERY B 118 GOOD	(1) (2) JUL 1945
6 do	VERY 212 GOOD	VERY 212 OD	(1) (2)

R 249273

† In Engineers' Books insert Horse Power. In Wireless Operators' Books insert gross tonnage and wireless classification of Ship.

John Harding-Dennis, the sixteen-year-old Second Radio Officer of the SS Empire Panther *(Harding-Dennis)*

SS Dorset *under aerial attack making the Malta run in August 1942*

DEMS gunners man the 6-inch gun mounted on a merchantman's stern

A Bofors provides anti-aircraft protection for an oil-tanker

U-boat officers hunt for targets (Ullstein)

Above: Springbank *before: The Bank Line freighter pictured at Cape Town before the war. Below:* Springbank *after: equipped with four twin 4-inch dual purpose high angle/low angle guns and a Fairey Fulmar catapult fighter. The* Springbank *was sunk while protecting Convoy* HG 43 *in September 1941* (Bank Line)

Shellfire damage to the Springbank's *sister ship the MV* Arranbank (Bank Line)

members some hope of survival, and within a further twenty-four hours they had accounted also for the *U-574*, commanded by Oberleutnant Gegnalbach – three submarines sunk on a single sortie, and at a time when the U-boat force was thought to be in total command of the Atlantic. As if to prove the brains behind the brawn, Walker, at a subsequent Admiralty meeting, became one of the first front line sailors of substance to stress the paramount importance of aircraft, land-based and carrier-based, in the protection of the convoys from the German submarines.

One important aspect of Walker's battle technique was the effect it had on the morale of the merchantmen sailing under his Group's protection. In an arena of hunter and hunted he was quintessentially the aggressor, and if occasionally he might be accused of leaving his charges temporarily unattended in his relentless pursuit of any U-boat venturing into the vicinity, this was more than counter-balanced by the sight of the escort ships tracking back and forth, hour after hour, following an asdic contact and periodically blanketing an area of sea with their depth charges. Quite frequently he made his kill, but that was by no means the only value of his constant foraging. U-boats twisting, turning, and submerging in their efforts to evade pursuers were in no state or position to press home a co-ordinated attack on their own account, and the tactics of the Escort Group were gaining the precious elements of time and distance for their convoys.

One such action concerned convoy *HG 84*, that set off homeward bound from Gibraltar on 9 June 1942, consisting of twenty merchant ships led by Commodore H.T. Hudson, RNR, in the 1,346 ton steamer *Pelavo*. In addition to the four escorts under Walker's command, the convoy included two merchant vessels with specific extra duties and equipment; the *Empire Morn* was a CAM-ship (Catapult Aircraft Merchantman) carrying a Hurricane fighter that could be used only for a single one-way sortie that would end with the pilot ditching close to the parent vessel in the hope of being picked up, while in the rear of the convoy the *Copeland* had been designated as a rescue ship and fitted out accordingly with medical and surgical supplies and extra bedding for wounded or exhausted survivors. Three more ships were due to join the convoy on 12 June at a rendezvous off the coast of Portugal.

These newcomers were in fact to constitute an added hazard, for they were shadowed all the way from Lisbon by a high-flying Focke-Wulf FW 200, and from the moment of their arrival every man on the convoy knew that a U-boat attack, sooner or later, was now inevitable. In the afternoon a submarine was heard signalling its first sighting, and an hour later it was spotted on the surface ten miles directly ahead of *HG 84*. As Walker in his sloop *Stork* set out to close the gap, his three corvettes operated independently to sweep the danger area around the merchantmen, and until after midnight it seemed that their efforts had been handsomely rewarded. The situation then was that not one but three U-boats had been held at bay, and not a ship had been lost.

Then, because of a minor and perhaps unavoidable miscalculation, everything changed dramatically and tragically in a matter of minutes. The corvette *Marigold* failed by some fifteen minutes to rejoin the convoy as instructed at one a.m., and in that short space of time the enemy found the gap they were looking for in the defensive screen. Their initial attack was devastating. The Commodore ship, the *Pelavo*, was simply blown out of the water by the first torpedo, and she was followed almost immediately by the *Etrib* (1,943 tons) and the *Slendal*, a foreign vessel of similar tonnage. For some three hours after this the convoy went unmolested, but the U-boats were merely re-grouping and positioning themselves for another onslaught from a different quarter.

It came at 4.30 in the morning of the 15th, and again the torpedoes found their marks. First to go was the *Thurso* (2,436 tons); loaded with munitions, she simply disintegrated in a blinding sheet of flame. Less horrifyingly spectacular, but no less final, was the fate a few seconds later of the *City of Oxford* (2,759 tons) which took a torpedo in one of the cargo-holds, rolled over on her side, and sank swiftly. In the convoy there was at this time something dangerously close to panic and, temporarily without an effective Commodore, the merchant ships started firing off batteries of snowflake rockets which made the whole grim scene as bright as day. For some reason they were not made to pay the obvious price of their folly – perhaps the U-boats were at the end of a long patrol and were short of torpedoes, or maybe their commanders were simply content to rest upon laurels obtained without loss; in either case the convoy was not subjected to any further attack.

Now the corvette HMS *Marigold* once again entered the action, and this time in altogether happier circumstances than before. Sent astern by Walker after the second U-boat attack to help the *Copeland* in the work of rescue, she eventually reappeared with her decks almost awash. Small wonder; on this tiny ship were no less than one hundred and seventy two survivors, many times the strength of her own ship's company. Walker ordered these men transferred to the *Copeland*, and *Marigold*, bobbing upon the water, became a warship once more.

Although there were no more submarine attacks, there were still U-boats between *HG 84* and her destination, the Clyde, and during the next few days Johnnie Walker was in fact to claim two of them as "probables". There was a final incident of high excitement, too, on 19 June, the last full day of the voyage, when a flight of German bombers were seen flying directly towards the convoy. They never reached their target. In their path, purely by chance, was the destroyer *Wild Swan*, a veteran of the 1914-18 war, which engaged them with such murderously sustained and accurate fire that she accounted for six of them, sending the three survivors scudding for home, before signalling almost laconically that she herself was sinking fast by the stern. For this action her captain, Commander C.E. Slater, RN, was awarded the Distinguished Service Order.

If Walker suffered any misgivings as to his superiors' reaction to his temerity in carrying the fight to the enemy with such a small force at his disposal, his mind was very soon to be put at rest. These men were well aware of what he had achieved; a sustained and well-planned attack on *HG 84* had been fought off for the loss of only five merchant vessels and one Hurricane fighter, and against that could reasonably be set the two U-boats he had claimed as "probables", for Walker could never have been accused of reporting kills on anything less than strong circumstantial evidence. All losses are tragic, but this after all was war in one of its most dangerous theatres, and on balance the tactics of the 36th Escort Group had paid handsome dividends.

After a six-month spell ashore during which he continued to evolve offensive schemes against the U-boats and to urge their acceptance upon his own Commander-in-Chief, Admiral Sir Max Horton, and upon the Admiralty, Walker returned to sea as commander of the Second Escort Group, his six sloops constituting a more powerful variation on his previous force of corvettes. They carried the war into the Bay of Biscay where, backed up now by regular air patrols flown by the Sunderlands of Coastal Command, they not only scored direct successes by sinking but also, by patrolling the approaches to the main U-boat bases in Lorient and Bordeaux, they forced the enemy to waste both time and fuel by spending long periods submerged. Whilst this naturally served to ease the pressure on the convoys, the Allied shipping losses, especially on the transatlantic runs, were still a source of great anxiety, and it was not for some considerable time, in fact not until the Spring of 1943, that the tide of fortune indisputably began to turn. By then Walker and his men had extended their operations to the Atlantic battle, and they continued to function very effectively, but also by then the whole scale of the Allied counter-offensive had hugely increased, and their work had become of less relative significance as simply a part of a greater pattern. No matter; they had already played a major part in helping to bring this new and improved situation into being.

1943 had in fact started very badly for the Allies, at least so far as the Battle of the Atlantic was concerned. On land things looked more hopeful, for the British and American armies had bottled Rommel in Tunisia while a Germany Army in Russia had surrendered at Stalingrad and were suffering the effects of the heroic resistance and counter-attack that was being thrown against them. But at sea the slaughter of the merchantmen was appalling, and in March of that year the losses inflicted by the U-boats on British shipping alone amounted to 384,898 tons, the highest monthly total of the entire war. The ships of the Americans and other Allies suffered proportionately, and this was the moment above all others when it seemed that Admiral Dönitz might well, after all, succeed in cutting the lifeline between Britain and the United States and, by extension, bring to an end the Arctic convoys upon which the Russians depended so desperately for the armour, the fuel, and the other resources with which to fling back the German armies on the Eastern Front.

April was another bad month for the Merchant Navy with the loss of a further 194,247 tons, but in May the Allies launched an unparalleled counter-attack based upon massive co-operation between surface craft, submarines, land-based aircraft and seaplanes, and Dönitz's command suffered a crushing defeat from which it was never to recover. In just four weeks the Germans lost forty-one ocean-going U-boats and many of their most experienced commanders, and though they hit back briefly in July, sinking 187,750 tons of British shipping, they never achieved anything remotely like that success again. That was almost the swan-song of the U-boat. The long and bitter Battle of the Atlantic had been lost and won. The troops and the supplies came pouring in from America, the convoys sailed to Murmansk and Archangel with no repetition of the horrors that had gone before, and just one year later the seas had been swept clear for the invasion of Europe.

Chapter 13

CONVOY *SC 42*: 1941

The successes of the escort groups during the summer months of 1941 had given Admiral Dönitz pause for thought, and by early autumn he had relocated the main strength of his U-boat force in lines patrolling the northern waters between Iceland and Greenland. There they lay in wait, eager and impatient, and on 9 September their tactics brought their reward.

The convoy they sighted that day was the *SC 42* out of Sydney, Cape Breton, seventy merchantmen escorted by the 24th Escort Group, one destroyer and three corvettes of the Royal Canadian Navy led by Commander J.C. Hibbard, RCN. One of these merchantmen was the SS *Empire Panther*, 5,600 tons, her 2nd Radio Officer was a sixteen-year old named John Harding-Dennis.

Young Harding-Dennis at that time was already a veteran, a survivor who had tasted salt water. He had taken the P.M.G's Special Certificate of Proficiency in Wireless Telegraphy in May 1940, and in October of that year he had been pitchforked from a boarding school background into active service on board the SS *Eskdene*, 3,829 tons. He is now himself the headmaster of a boarding school on Humberside, and he talks with feeling of these early, impressionable days. "My father had immediately gone into the army, my mother into the nursing services; intensely patriotic, they were pleased, I think, that I had joined up.

"The Chief Radio Officer's welcoming smile flickered for a moment and went out. He stared unbelievingly up and down all five feet two of me, slowly taking in the brand-new uniform, the untarnished gold braid, the lost look. 'Jesus Christ' he muttered, 'they're kidnapping the poor little sods now'."

"My quarters weren't exactly the Ritz. Two iron-framed bunks slotted into the bulkhead one above the other, both draped in faded pink cotton bedspreads, a settee with two drawers under it, a tip-up washbasin and slop-bucket, a carafe half full of dirty water, a narrow wardrobe at the foot of the settee – all lit by a smoky oil-lamp on gimbals and vastly overheated by a small bogey stove with a black pipe that glowed in the shadows and took *most* of the smoke out through a hole in the deckhead. Everything in that cabin was covered by a layer of coaldust. I sank down on the settee and fought hard to keep back the tears. Percy F. Westerman had not prepared me for this; *his* young heroes were almost piped aboard when they joined their first ship.

"Suddenly the door opened and a cheerful face peered in. 'Hello; new Sparks aren't you? I'm just across the alley-way. Come on over and have a cup of cocoa and a chat.' The cocoa and his wife's fruit cake worked wonders. We talked about books and stamps and ships and foreign ports, and just before I left he lent me his own copy, one his wife had just given him, of *The Herries Chronicle*, a book I love to this day. As long as I live I shall always remember the kindness shown me by that 3rd Mate.

"After that it was all plain sailing – well, almost. The CRO treated me with amused tolerance, but made sure I learned my job and carried it out. Life at sea was exciting, and I was always asking questions of everyone who was prepared to answer them. Eventually the whole ship's company seemed to have adopted me as its kid brother, and I had the devil's own job at times to escape into the seamier sides of Buenos Aires, Rosario, and Colon.

"Our only armament on that first trip was an old shoulder Lewis, and the captain was so concerned about my safety that he ordered me to stay out of sight whenever enemy aircraft were spotted. Once, though, we were attacked off the East coast when I was on bridge signalling watch and unable to carry out that order. To my delight I was able to watch the whole action, too excited to feel any fear, too inexperienced to sense any need for it.

"Fear came later, much later, when constant tension, fed by harrowing memories and the ghosts of lost ships, had wearied the spirit and strung out every nerve. It came in the danger zones when you were alone, lying fully clothed on the bunk, with life jacket, seaboots, and skinning-out bag always in reach. Then, the slightest bang – a steel door clanging shut, a dropped spanner in the engine-room – would make you jump up in a panic of sweat. You imagined the torpedo track heading for you straight amidships, and in your mind's eye you saw the blinding flash of the explosion that would blow a hole as big as a house below your cabin and blast you clean through the deckhead.

"The torpedo struck on the port side, abreast of the forward well-deck, and the *Eskdene* lurched heavily to starboard, canting the wireless room's swivel chair sharply over and dumping me far from ceremoniously on the deck. A glance at the brass wall-clock told me it was 04.07 hrs: the familiar thump-thump of the engine had been replaced by eerie creaks and, more ominously, a loud and constant rumbling from deep down in the bowels of the ship. The bridge voice-pipe whistled, then "Okay, Sparks – get cracking." Within seconds I had the rheostat hard over and was tapping out a distress call; SOS SOS SOS, followed by our call sign and position and ending with the words 'torpedoed and sinking.' "The 1st Mate shoved his head round the door. 'The main aerial's gone.' I switched to the emergency, continuing to transmit, and shortly afterwards the Chief Radio Officer tapped me on the shoulder. He had taken a bad blow on the head and was still groggy, but he gave me an encouraging grin: 'All right, Tich; I'll take over now. Better shove off, or you'll miss the boat.' The starboard boat was already in the water as I waited my turn by the falls, when I realised I'd not brought any cigarettes; I slithered down the ladder to my cabin and raced back again just as she was fending off. I had five hundred State Express 555 in my fist, and as things turned out, they came in handy. We hauled away, and after a while a great cheer went up as the port lifeboat rounded the stern to join us and a check told us that not one man was missing.

"A flash away to starboard gave us our first glimpse of the U-boat as she fired her gun and the second torpedo that sent the *Eskdene* hissing head first to the bottom. No-one spoke. For a long time we just sat gazing at the spot where she went down. Then sadly, and still in silence, we stepped the mast, hoisted the sail, and set course for land."

It was with his sixteenth birthday just one month past that the 2nd Radio Officer of the *Empire Panther* watched the U-boat pack close in on Convoy *SC 42*, and realised that once again he was in deep waters. At first, tucked in the middle of some seventy ships covering 18 square sea miles in 13 columns, he felt that his ship might be relatively immune from enemy attack. He did not know then – none of them did – that they had already been infiltrated, by no less than seventeen submarines. They were soon to learn.

"Our sense of security was badly shaken when U-boats at periscope depth began to cruise at will down the lines of the convoy, actually amongst us, selecting their targets with studied nonchalance. First to go was the SS *Muneric* with a cargo of iron ore; the estimated sinking time for an ore carrier was fifty seconds. One such freighter, stationed just ahead of us in the port column got the hammer too, in broad daylight. As we sailed on past her, just two cables away, she sank like a stone, with no time to launch a lifeboat nor even a raft – there could have been no survivors. The *Gypsum Queen*, in the port column too, was different. We watched fascinated as, with her engines still running, and keeping perfect station, she slowly sank lower and lower in the water until, finally, her masts and her trunk just vanished from sight. It was *weird*.

"In the morning, one of the Prince Line ships was torpedoed; the crew, very calmly, lowered the boats and pulled away. Then we spotted her captain leaving his cabin on the lower bridge, watched as he threw the confidential papers overboard in their weighted canvas bag, shepherded his black Labrador into the jolly boat, and with his briefcase tucked under the arm of his best shore-going suit, unhurriedly lowered away and pulled clear of his sinking ship. We felt better immediately.

"The night attacks were pretty bad. When you'd been at actions almost round the clock for three days and nights, with no sleep and precious little food, the tendency was to jump at every sound as you strained through the darkness with a pair of indifferent night-glasses. The slightest glow or phosphorescence in the water brought an immediate shout from somewhere: 'torpedo starboard beam.' And always there were the booms and rumblings, the distress rockets going up, and the inevitable Snowflakes from the escorts, lighting up the whole damn convoy and bringing rich language from the officers on the bridge: 'That's right, you stupid bastards – give them a good target to aim at'." Snowflakes could only have been dreamed up by some bright bugger sitting snug behind a drawing-board.

"It was pitch dark when the ship abeam of us in the starboard column went up with a tremendous flash and blew us on the bridge clean off our feet. She was carrying munitions – there were no survivors; she didn't launch any boats.

"But worst of all was the sight of a tanker going up, burning like the pit, wreathed in a pall of black, greasy smoke – the light from that one gave the U-boat all the help it needed to finish her off. We watched as men threw themselves overboard, often into patches of burning oil; a few had the presence of mind to swim under water before surfacing in a dark patch, but when we picked them up later they just lay on the saloon floor, in alleyways, on the open deck, retching and convulsing with their lungs full of oil. There were scrambling nets slung from the side of every ship, and few of us failed to pick up at least some of these poor devils.

"We had started out as fourth ship in our column: by the third day we were in the lead. That night we saw a U-boat gliding like a ghost across our bows; the Old Man clung to the bridge dodger and nearly ruptured himself trying to ram her, but she was too fast for us, and she slid quietly away into the darkness. Then the fog came down, blanketing us from further attack, the ships scattered to avoid collision, and we put on full speed ahead and made our way independently to Loch Ewe."

The almost continuous hammering to which Convoy *SC 42* was subjected lasted, not for a matter of hours, but for days and nights on end. The first submarine was sighted in the early hours of 9 September, the *Muneric* went down the following day, and the attack was built up and pursued relentlessly until the surviving ships crept thankfully under a blanket of fog late on 15 September. To add to the tension, the constant strain upon reserves of courage and resource, throughout these interminable days and nights the sea across which they were crawling, often at a pitiful 3 knots, was littered with rafts and wreckage and the human evidence, alive and no longer alive, of the fate each man among them had reason to expect as his own.

Almost from the outset the convoy never had a chance, and yet, under the appalling circumstance of war, no blame can reasonably be attached for what became of it. In the early days of the voyage the weather was atrocious, easterly gales driving down its speed to less than half the anticipated 7½ knots and for forty-eight nerve-racking hours preventing it from making any headway whatsoever. Then, on 8 September, an Admiralty intelligence report of U-boat activity led to a decision, logical enough, to change course towards Greenland – and the new course led them straight down the throats of the waiting wolf-pack.

For a long while the luck ran all with the attackers. The Canadian Escort Group, three corvettes spearheaded by the destroyer HMCS *Skeena*, inadequate in both fire-power and numbers, was lacking also in hard experience, and the battle that confronted them was something entirely new. The enemy, suddenly, was in among them; evasive action carried dire risk of collision; ships were going down on every quarter, and the rash of signals flying back and forth between the escorts had all the verbose uncertainty of beginners. Harding-Dennis, with unaccustomed bitterness, remarks scathingly of this: "Professional seamen, certificated officers who had served their time, took less than kindly to being talked down to by some wavy-navy ex-shop assistant dressed up in a little brief authority."

The scene, in short, was pure Hieronymus Bosch, and its horror was compounded by the escort's hellish dilemma in facing up to the necessary choice between immediacy and compassion. In the event, compassion won. After hours and hours of heartbreaking and fruitless tail-chasing, while the U-boats coolly picked off their victims, Commander Hibbard sent the corvettes astern to pick up survivors, and the convoy sailed on with only *Skeena* to protect it.

Assistance, and the first successful action carried out by *SC42*'s escorts against the U-boats, came dramatically, and from a totally unexpected source. What effect it had upon the mission as a whole there is of course no means of telling, but it must have worked wonders for morale, and certainly it underlined heavily the inestimable value of training, teamwork, and experienced leadership. Commander J.D. Prentice, R.N.(Rtd.), along with a team of R.N. asdic operators, had been seconded to the Royal Canadian Navy for instructional purposes, and the situation developing south of Greenland seemed to him an irresistible opportunity for giving a practical turn to the instruction. With the blessings of authority he took his two corvettes, HMCS *Chambly* and *Moosejaw*, out of harbour in Newfoundland, and set off to intercept. That was on 5 September.

At around midnight on 10 September, having drilled his young crews exhaustively throughout the intervening days, Prentice closed the scene of the attack, and swung immediately into action. One of his instructional team, manning the asdic, reported a definite submarine contact; a young Lieutenant on his first voyage took steady charge of the depth-charge crew, and within seconds the *U-501* came boiling to the surface, to be summarily dispatched by the *Chambly* with its gun and the *Moosejaw* with its hull. The rest of the wolf-pack continued to attack, and five more merchantmen were torpedoed and sunk – but the *SC42*, at last, had drawn blood. Next day another submarine was accounted for, and the convoy limped wearily into

Home waters, the survivors secure, but fifteen of their companion ships at the bottom.

Chapter 14

ENDURANCE

When the liner *City of Cairo* (8,034 tons) was torpedoed at 8.30 p.m. on 6 November 1942, homeward bound and five days after leaving Cape Town, three passengers and eighteen members of her crew were killed in the explosion. In comparison to the majority of the immediate survivors, those twenty-one may be regarded as the lucky ones.

The second torpedo to strike had smashed several of the life-boats, and within seconds scores of men, women, and children were swimming for their lives. That ordeal, in most cases, was not to last for very long, because the master, Captain Rogerson, the Chief Officer, Mr Britt, and a number of Quartermasters and other experienced seamen had all survived, and the cool, methodical conduct of the initial rescue operation was testimony to their training, discipline, and personal courage. These same qualities, it must be added, were at once exhibited to an admirable degree by a number of the civilian passengers, and especially by the women and children.

In the badly damaged No 1 life-boat, for example, which was down to the gunwales, leaking, and littered with broken, tangled gear, it was explained that if some of the passengers would go overboard and either cling to the boat or else support themselves on the nearest floating wreckage, the crew members would bale out the boat and clear up the mess in a matter of minutes. The first to go were a titled English lady and her three young children, who slipped over the side without a murmur and swam to an empty fuel tank that was drifting nearby. Others followed their example, and despite intermittent swamping caused by the rolling swell, the life-boat was soon seaworthy.

Throughout that night the No 1 boat, temporarily under the command of Quartermaster Angus MacDonald, moved around picking up survivors from rafts and wreckage, and some who were relying solely upon their life-jackets. By dawn the boat was full, and soon, as the work of rescue went on, it was dangerously overloaded. Among those picked up were Quartermaster Bob Ironside, a particular friend of MacDonald's, and the Chief Officer, Sidney

Britt, who naturally took over command of the boat and responsibility for its occupants' safety. His first act was to hold a shouted conference with Captain Rogerson, who was in another boat, and their decisions were both logical and humane. They would make for the island of St. Helena, five hundred miles to the north; and since Britt's boat was leaking badly and had damaged its rudder and lost half of its water supply, all the children on board should be transferred, in exchange for adult volunteers. With this accomplished, and with families re-united, the survivors hoisted sail and set course.

After two days in reasonably favourable winds it became clear that Britt's boat, despite the leaking and the damage, was making better headway, and it was decided in a further conference with Captain Rogerson that they should make their best speed and, when they reached St Helena, alert and direct the rescue services. And so the No 1 boat moved on ahead, and by next day had lost sight of Captain Rogerson and their other ship-mates; they were never seen again. The Chief Officer and Quartermaster MacDonald took stock of the situation and tried to organise their resources, which proved no simple, straightforward task.

With fifty-four survivors aboard – twenty-three Europeans, including three women, and thirty-one lascars – the boat was so overcrowded that they had to take turns at sitting down to rest. Worse than that, of all the men aboard, only a small number were willing to pull their weight in the battle for continued survival. The lascars, with two honourable exceptions in the old engine-room Serang and a fireman from Zanzibar, lapsed at once into total apathy and simply lay praying to Allah in the bottom of the boat, sometimes in more than a foot of water, while the Europeans sat, stood, or tried to work around them. And some of those Europeans showed little more spirit and resilience than the lascars. Besides those there were the injured, who were helpless and useless through no fault of their own. Quartermaster Ironside had hurt his back badly in the explosion and was virtually unable to move or even to sit up. Miss Taggart, a stewardess, was also severely injured and had to be laid flat in a place found for her in the bows. There was a doctor on board, Dr Taskar, but he had suffered the most severe mental and moral collapse of them all, and though physically unhurt he proved incapable even in assisting with the bandaging of the wounded.

In contrast, however, there were those whose courage and sheer spirit can be described only as heroic, and outstanding among these was the youngest passenger of all, Diana Jarman, a girl of twenty whose utter selflessness and steadfast refusal to flinch were to prove the most shining example of all throughout the ordeal that lay ahead. Another who handled himself well was Robert Watts, an aeronautical engineer from Reading, who cheerfully applied his skills and his muscle to any and every practical problem that was put to him. And above all, there was Quartermaster Angus MacDonald.

A harbinger of what was in store for them came as early as the second night, when Dr Taskar began calling loudly "Boy – bring me more coffee", and was later found to have cut a large piece out of a sleeping companion's trousers in order to repair a rip in his own. MacDonald quietly relieved the doctor of his pocket-knife, which he later treasured for many years as a grim souvenir. During the fourth night Dr Taskar simply gave up the ghost, and the company observed the sombre ritual of a simple prayer and consignment of the body to the deep, the first and most formal of their burials at sea.

As the days passed with long periods of flat calm and no sign of rescue, others began to fail, and inevitably the first to die were those who had done nothing, physically or morally, to help either themselves or others. On the sixth morning three lascars were found dead on the bottom, and during the seventh night Miss Taggart, whose enforced stillness wrapped in sodden, salt-caked clothes had reduced her body to a mass of sores, slipped from her position and fell on top of another passenger, a civilian homeward bound from Calcutta. Neither rose again, and at dawn on the eighth day they were cast over the side, along with several more of the lascars. The water boiled behind the boat as shoals of sharks fought over the grisly feast.

A week stretched interminably to a fortnight, and each day the life-boat rose higher in the water as its human cargo was reduced. The lascars began dying like flies; a British engineer, young and healthy, sat motionless for two days with his chin on his chest, lacking the spirit to fight back even when chided by MacDonald to take a good look at Diana Jarman, who was suffering as much as anyone but who remained cheerful and uncomplaining and who spent most of her waking hours at the tiller. The lad tried half-heartedly, but not for long, and very soon he too was put over the side. A stewardess, Annie Crouch, had similarly declined, refusing to budge from the water-slopping bottom of the boat, where her feet and legs had swollen hideously, and on the tenth day she was released from her misery, leaving Diana Jarman as the only woman in the boat.

Now even men strong in character and physique began to fall. Chief Officer Britt's mind began to wander, and the last few entries in the daily log he had been keeping were later found to be incomprehensible gibberish; he was laid alongside the injured Bob Ironside, who was failing fast and whose only thoughts were for his wife and baby daughter at home in Aberdeen. On the fourteenth morning big Robert Watts, who had worked tirelessly and with never a word of complaint, was found dead in his seat, and was buried along with six others who had not survived the night. Next day both Sidney Britt and Bob Ironside succumbed, along with three other Europeans and most of the remaining lascars. One fireman, unable to stand the strain any longer, jumped overboard. He forgot to remove his life-jacket, and the sharks got to him before he could drown.

On the seventeenth night came another macabre incident. A shout from Diana Jarman awoke Angus MacDonald to the realisation that the boat was half full of water, and examination showed that the plug-hole was open. Hastily shoving in a spare bung, with the help of others he managed to bale out successfully – but within thirty minutes the same thing had happened again. Again he replaced the plug, and again he baled out the boat, but this time he lay down to rest with one eye open. Half an hour later he watched a young European stretch out a hand to the plug-hole. Asked why he had tried to sink the boat, the young man could manage no more worthy explanation than "I'm going to die, so we might as well all go together." He did die, the very next day – but not before he had managed to snatch all the contents of the medicine chest and throw them over the side.

By the end of the third week, of the fifty-four men and women who had set out for St Helena only eight were still alive, and even that pitiful number was soon to be reduced. Three of them died in a single night, leaving only Angus MacDonald, steward Jack Edmead, seaman Joe Green, the old engine-room Serang, and Diana Jarman, herself now very sick with a tortured throat and a dribble of thick yellow phlegm oozing constantly from her mouth; yet still, in a whisper, she managed to speak encouragingly and even cheerfully to the others. Joe Green, too, showed his quality, though in a different way. One night – they had by now lost count – he refused to take his place in the bottom of the boat, but laid himself instead across the stern, saying simply "I won't last the night, and you'd never manage to lift me over the side." He was dead next morning, and so was the old serang.

The three survivors now drifted aimlessly about the ocean for days on end, unable to work the boat but still helping each other in small but significant ways. A word of hope, a wash given in salt water, MacDonald recounting to Diana his dreams of home, the girl squeezing streams of pus from the arm MacDonald had poisoned days earlier in his fierce and successful battle to capture and kill a three-foot dog-fish that had thrown itself into the boat. One night, at last, it rained, and they were able to drink the bitter water they collected in the salt-caked sail. Their spirits soared, and they began to feel real hope, but they had three more days and nights to endure before they heard the sound they scarcely dared to believe, the beat of a diesel engine.

It was dark, and MacDonald feverishly struck one of the life-boat matches. At once there was a shout. "All right, put that light out: can you come alongside?" Incredibly, they succeeded; with Diana at the tiller these two emaciated men heaved on the oars and brought the lifeboat to the dark outline they could see looming across the water. A line was thrown and MacDonald made fast; a ladder was lowered and two men came scrambling down. Diana and Edmead were carried aboard the rescue ship; MacDonald, proud and self-reliant to the end, climbed the rope ladder unaided.

The ship that had picked them up was the German *Rhakotis*, but they were far beyond caring about nationality, and in fact they were very well treated. One of the first questions they were asked was when they had been torpedoed, and when they replied "6th November" there was a moment of silence before the German captain said, speaking slowly, "It is now 12th December." Five weeks. A cabin was alloted to the two men and Diana was put to bed in the sick bay, where they were not allowed to visit her for several days, although the captain gave them regular reports as to her progress. She was unable to swallow any solid nourishment, and was being fed intravenously.

On the fifth day aboard the *Rhakotis* the captain and the ship's doctor told them that this could not continue much longer, and asked their permission to operate to clear the congestion and relieve the inflammation in her throat. They agreed, since obviously the doctor was best qualified to decide what was necessary, and for the first time they were taken to see her. Apart, inevitably, from being very thin she looked well, and spoke to them cheerfully though in a whisper. Her hair had been shampooed and set and her morale, as always, was high. Relieved, they left her and went away.

They saw her again at seven o'clock that evening – just half an hour after she had died. The operation, they were told, had been successful, but the strain of anaesthesia had proved too much for her tired and damaged heart. She looked peaceful and serene lying there with the white bandage at her throat. The two survivors turned away in silence, unable to speak, and, in the words of Angus MacDonald, "I turned into my bunk and cried like a baby all night. It was the first time I had broken down since the whole thing started, and I think it was the same with Jack." Diana was buried next morning with full Naval honours, the ship stopped, the crew drawn up in uniform, the coffin draped in the Union Jack, and Angus MacDonald and Jack Edmead were not the only men present who wept over the grave.

The end of the story of Diana Jarman was not, however, the end of the story of these two British merchant seamen; their powers of endurance had still to be tested to the limit. The *Rhakotis* was bound for Bordeaux, where she was due to arrive on New Year's Day. After a Christmas Day on which, as Angus MacDonald wryly remarked, he fed and fared better as a German prisoner than did most free seamen on British ships, there was rising excitement as the ship approached its destination, reaching its peak on New Year's Eve with the news that a rendezvous had been arranged with four U-boats that would escort them into port.

At four-thirty p.m. on New Year's Day, when crew and prisoners were enjoying a celebratory dinner, the alarm bells sounded, there was a thunderous barrage of gun-fire, and all hands were ordered instantly to the boats. They were under attack by a British cruiser. She was firing salvos, and by the time they had cleared the *Rhakotis* she was ablaze from stem to stern; the cruiser continued to fire, and within minutes the German ship was sinking.

Angus MacDonald was in the port life-boat with thirty-four others including a few other prisoners, though none of them was British. It was not until years later he was to learn that his friend Jack Edmead, in the starboard boat, had eventually made his way to Spain, and thence to England, only to lose his life on the next ship he joined when she too was torpedoed.

MacDonald sat it out with his captors and fellow-prisoners until the following morning when, despite the heavy seas in the Bay of Biscay, their captain decided to risk a run straight for the coast of France. The gamble paid off, and a few hours later there was a great shout from the men as a periscope was sighted and, within minutes, a U-boat came to the surface alongside them. Under orders from its commander they made the transfer and settled into their new quarters, each man as he came aboard finding thrust into his hand a large mug of steaming coffee well laced with rum. They were then shown where to lie, and to lie still, for this was only a small boat on its way home from a fourteen-day patrol and with thirty-five extra passengers it was now packed like a tin of sardines.

The relief of the survivors lasted for just fifteen minutes before once again they heard the clamour of alarm bells, and the submarine's nose dipped in a crash-dive. Three explosions, close, closer, and right alongside, followed immediately as they were depth-charged by an aircraft of Coastal Command, Royal Air Force, flying a routine patrol over the Bay. The men were thrown all over each other, the engines were stopped, and for an hour they lay still and silent before daring to creep their way once more towards Bordeaux. The air was becoming increasingly foul, and at length the captain decided to surface, open the conning-tower hatch, and let fresh air flood the boat. This respite also enabled the cook to rustle up a hot meal for everyone, and it was in good spirits that they submerged once again to steal their way to home and safety. They learned that now, because of the British air blockade over Bordeaux, they were making instead for St Nazaire.

It was noon on 3 January when the bells sounded again, this time not the alarm, but action stations. The crew moved swiftly to their posts and MacDonald, lying close to the torpedo tubes, had the eerie and disturbing experience of learning that he was engaged, by proxy as it were, in stalking a British destroyer. He was still pondering the strangeness of his predicament when the bells jangled out the alarm and the situation changed swiftly and dramatically yet again.

"The nose of the sub went down at a terrific speed as she crash-dived, and she seemed to be standing on her head. The suspense was terrible, and then came the first explosion. We were still going down, but not so steeply, and gradually we seemed to settle on an even keel. With the second and third explosions we were thrown all over the place, and as the boat jumped and rolled from side to side all the lights went out. There was a bump, and we reckoned we had hit bottom. We could still hear the depth-charges, but they seemed to be drawing further away each time. There was not a sound now in our compartment, and we lay deathly still for literally hours with the air getting fouler and fouler and everyone slowly suffocating. An Under-officer warned us not to speak or move, or we would use up what little air was left. No water was coming into our for'ard compartment, but no orders were coming in either, and we could only lie there and choke and wonder what had gone wrong amidships or aft. I thought 'after all I've been through, what a hell of a way to go – suffocating in a German submarine, depth-charged by a British destroyer.''

Angus MacDonald's fears, happily, were not to be realised. First came a hammering, in code, from the far side of the bulkhead, and then the water-tight door was opened. Repairs were carried out during the rest of the night, and at daybreak the submarine rose slowly to the surface, opened the hatches, and let the fresh air come blessedly rushing in. At noon on 4 January 1943 they slid gently into the U-boat pens at St Nazaire. For the German crew there was a rapturous reception from a military band and a cluster of high-ranking officers. For Quartermaster Angus MacDonald, survivor extraordinary, there was interrogation, a train journey to Wilhelmshaven, and the prospect of two years and four months as a Merchant Navy prisoner of war in Milag Nord.

Chapter 15

A "VERY ORDINARY BLOKE": 1942

Ron Lang, born on 11 October 1928, one of fourteen children in a family living in a Torquay Council house, describes himself with obvious sincerity and almost with apology as a 'very ordinary bloke'. He then, under persuasion, lists some of the activities and occupations that so far have constituted his very ordinary life.

"I've been married seven times, I helped in the cleaning up at Aberfan. I've been an errand boy for butchers, grocers, and chemists, and I was a driver for a long time – taxis, tippers, and trucks, long-distance runs with rigids and articulated, and for a while I drove a Mobile Cinerama around England, Scotland, and Wales. Then of course I was driving again in the RASC before being switched to the Pioneer Corps.

"For a year or two I travelled with the fairs and circuses, fighting in the booths; two of my best pals then were Freddie Mills and Randy Turpin. Course I never had to tackle them, thank God – I was a lightweight – but I used to spar with them a lot. Great blokes, both of them, and of course both of them gone. A whole lot of my old mates are gone, come to think of it – but that's another story"

That other story concerns the years Ron Lang spent as a merchant seaman, and it started in a rage of grief and determination over the loss of an idolised, eighteen-year old brother, killed in action manning his gun on H.M.S. *Albatross*.

"When he used to come home on leave he always had time for me, and he taught me to play the harmonica. First tune I ever learned from him was: 'The Red River Valley', and d'you know, I can hear every note of it to this day. Then my mother got the telegram. Well, I took his name – I'm not Ron at all really, not on my birth certificate – and I stuck a couple of years on my age and joined the Merchant Navy in Plymouth, about thirty miles down the coast. I was about four feet nothing, but they were hard up by then, and I got my first job as galley boy on the M.V. *Condee*. It was hard work and sometimes damn dirty, but I was happy – I'd run away to sea and I was going to win the war." Ron Lang was then thirteen years of age.

He was still four months short of his fourteenth birthday when he joined the *Ocean Freedom*, 7,173 tons, and embarked upon one of the most terrible voyages in maritime history. The *Ocean Freedom* was one of only 14 merchant vessels that survived out of the 36 that set out in 1942 on the run to Murmansk and Archangel as Convoy *PQ 17*.

It is chilling to see it through the eyes of a thirteen-year old boy. "I joined the *Ocean Freedom* in Iceland, where I'd landed from another ship, out of Ireland. I was glad to be getting away, as I thought, out of the bloody awful weather there – snow, fog, thick, swirling mists, ice, and always the bitter cold wind. It was exciting, too, all these ships, especially so many warships; I'd never seen anything like it, not even at the pictures. Then we set out, and I learned we were bound for some place in Russia called Murmansk. And I soon learned what weather can *really* be like when you're at sea. The water would freeze all over the ship and the decks were covered in thick sheets of ice; you had to be damn careful what you touched, and watch where you were standing if a sea was running. The rest of the convoy, with their rigging all encrusted with snow and ice, looked just like ghost ships in the fog. The crew, though, were a cheery lot, especially the cook. He was always whistling and singing, and he was very good to me – the food he dished up was fine and hot, and always plenty of it. I must say I never went hungry – but oh my God, it was *so* cold.

"It all started when we were four days out. On that day I did really think and feel I would never see my home or family again, as, I suppose, did many other men (*sic*) in that convoy. And it went on; every day the German Planes were bombing and strafing the ships, and nearly every time they hit some of them, starting fires and sinking some – it was really awful to watch. Especially at night-time, when you couldn't see very much, except the fires burning all around you and you knew another ship had been hit, gunfire exploding in the sky, everything all lit up for a while with the fires, big explosions then, and the fires going out, hissing. I didn't really know what was going on, and after those first few days I really got scared and frightened, I used to try and sleep in the galley at nights, for it did make me feel a bit safer to know I was not to be down below decks when our turn came. Things happened I never want to see or hear again – the noises in the night and the sights you saw all around you when it came day – you just couldn't describe it.

"Then it was 4 July, and the men were having a drink all day, whenever they got the chance. That was the day I had my very first drink, whisky, and truth is I didn't like it at all. I learned later it was a celebration, and what it was we were celebrating – I was growing up fast. Everyone was happy that day, until the news began to spread around the ship that the escorts, the Navy, were leaving us to ourselves.

"The men were very angry, shouting and cursing, even the Cook as well. I didn't understand what was wrong, really, but after a while, when I'd listened to the men talking, and even cookie swearing, I did become really frightened and knew we'd never get to wherever we were going and I'd never see my home again. And the planes kept coming and bombing, and the ships kept getting sunk. I was bombed many times later in the days, and I was sunk too, but, it was never again like that.

"After being at sea a long time, and getting bombed a lot, ships going down all around us, we came to some land and stayed for a while at anchor; then we left again, and the cook told me, when I asked him, that it wasn't very far to go now. But I saw things I'd never seen in my life before – icebergs – and we hit one and got damaged; I don't think I've ever prayed so much in my life. We kept getting bombed, and ships kept sinking, but we came to a big port in Russia, Archangel it was called. We were supposed to be going to Murmansk, but we'd been diverted, I was told. When we came in there were only a few other ships there, but all their sirens were blowing. More ships came in, not many, and they started unloading men who'd been sunk and wounded and some of them burned and blinded – it was awful. But we were there, though we weren't even allowed to go ashore, and I felt great – and then I remembered we had to go all the way back."

The full story of *PQ17* cannot be told here, for every man involved in it, from the then First Sea Lord, Admiral Sir Dudley Pound, down to the rawest galley boy, like Ron Lang, had his own adventure and his own tragedy.

The background to the sailing of the convoy was both military and political. From October 1941 to mid June 1942 sixteen convoys sailed and discharged at Archangel and Murmansk and up to March 1942 only one of 110 ships were lost. After March the days began to draw longer and the Germans sent the battleship *Tirpitz* and the heavy cruiser *Hipper* to Trondheim fjord. In March the *Tirpitz* attacked Convoy *PQ-12* but was driven off. *PQ-13* in April was severely mauled by aircraft, submarines and surface warships, losing five ships out of 19. The sending of another convoy looked like an invitation to disaster.

The British Government was under constant pressure from Stalin to maintain the traffic of the Arctic convoys throughout the summer months, and in view of the hardships with which the Soviet armies and indeed the Russian people as a whole were faced in 1942, it is hard to see how Churchill could have resisted these demands and still expected Britain to retain credibility as a loyal and trustworthy ally. The execution of this policy, however, was fraught with danger, and the officer directly responsible for the execution, Admiral Tovey, C-in-C Home Fleet, was loud in his protests to the First Sea Lord that it would inevitably lead to a major disaster. He pointed out repeatedly that not only would the almost continuous summer daylight in Arctic waters make secrecy of movement virtually impossible, but movement itself was still limited by the ice barrier north of Bear Island. The ships, claimed Tovey, once sighted, would be at the mercy of the German submarines and the German bomber squadrons stationed in northern Norway. Sir Dudley Pound repeated Tovey's objections to the Prime Minister and they were brushed aside in the interests of political expediency. And so although Pound, by his subseqent orders, was the man primarily responsible for the desertion and the destruction of *PQ 17*, it is reasonable to assume that he issued these orders with at least the implicit blessing of Winston Churchill.

He had the blessing also of the President of the United States, for Franklin Roosevelt was adamant, like the British Prime Minister, that the supplies to Russia should flow uninterrupted throughout the year. America was by this time sending vast quantities of arms and armour to the aid of the Soviet armies, and indeed of the merchant vessels that made up the *PQ 17* no less than two-thirds came from the United States, a circumstance that was to engender much understandable bitterness in that country in the years ahead, when the true facts regarding the convoy at last began to filter through, not least in 1945, when a large number of American survivors were finally repatriated, each with a grim and grisly tale to tell of desertion by the warships of the Royal Navy.

In relation to this "desertion" one survivor for whom one must feel enormous sympathy is Captain Jack Broome, RN (Rtd), the commander of the close escort of destroyers, whose action in leaving the convoy totally unprotected was at the very root of the merchant seamen's accusation and complaint. On the face of it such action was indefensible and contrary to all the traditions not only of the Royal Navy but of sailors of any breed at any time, when other sailors alongside them are seen to be in deadly danger. Broome seemed cast as the natural villain of the piece, and indeed was regarded as such by many until years later his conduct was completely vindicated in the Law Courts in a libel action that resulted in his being awarded very substantial damages. Close study of the relevant signals and documents, many of which have been released only recently, show beyond any shadow of doubt that his exoneration from blame was no more than an act of simple justice. The blame for the tragedy – and blame there undoubtedly was – lay elsewhere, and much higher up the ladder of authority.

The British and American elements of *PQ 17* gathered around Iceland under massive protection, initially, from the naval forces of Britain and the United States. The escort, consisting of several separate units with separate functions, with varying areas of reponsibility and under varying orders as to their actions under given sets of circumstance, was in fact a task force. The convoy was to be shadowed by two battleships, one aircraft carrier, three cruisers, and nine destroyers. There was in addition a squadron comprising six cruisers with a protective screen of seven accompanying destroyers, there were two submarines in attendance, and there was Broome's close escort force that included six destroyers, two corvettes, four asdic trawlers, and two anti-aircraft vessels. The importance of seeing the convoy and its cargo safely through to Murmansk had most certainly not been under-estimated by the naval officers who planned every detail of its protection.

Haunting the minds of both Churchill and Sir Dudley Pound, however, was the presence of the German battleship *Tirpitz* in Trondheim, northern Norway, and repeated intelligence reports from that country that she, possibly in company with the *Hipper* and the *Scheer*, was about to sail north-east to attack the convoy, of whose formation and intentions the German command was already fully aware, for security at every level had been lamentably lax.

It was a faulty Intelligence report, stating that *Tirpitz* and *Hipper* had left Trondheim on 3 July, that initiated the series of signals that led directly to the disaster. It had been decided at the Admiralty, no doubt quite rightly, that against such opposition the British and American capital ships could hold their own only in open water where the enemy was denied the support of land-based aircraft, and the First Sea Lord had no intention of risking his aircraft-carrier, his battleships and cruisers on the extreme reaches of the run, when the convoy would be within easy reach of the German-held Norwegian airfields. This was reasonable as well as prudent, and was understood by everyone, including the Merchant Navy captains, even before the long voyage had begun.

What was not understood and never will be condoned is that Sir Dudley Pound, notoriously reluctant at any time to delegate authority even to his most senior and competent subordinates, would have the arrogance to insist upon directing an undertaking of this magnitude from his underground operations-room at the Admiralty, and to do so over the heads of Admirals Tovey and Hamilton, commanding the battle fleet and the cruiser squadron. As if this were not misjudgement enough, Pound then made the beginner's error of failing to check the authenticity of the information upon which his subsequent orders were based. To meet the threat posed by the two German battleships the shadowing fleet was retained to patrol some three hundred and fifty miles behind the convoy, the cruisers were ordered to proceed westward with all possible speed to meet the threat of enemy surface action, and, in the third and most infamous executive signal, the convoy was ordered to scatter. Among the recipients of that signal was the commander of the escort destroyers, Jack Broome, who was faced with the choice – if it could be called a choice in relation to a seasoned officer of the Royal Navy – of obeying or ignoring an order recived direct from the First Sea Lord. He might indeed have disobeyed his orders, as he has always insisted he was sorely tempted to do, but he could not have saved the convoy, because from the moment the signal to scatter was hoisted on the commodore ship, the *River Afton*, the convoy, as such, simply ceased to exist, and each ship was under orders to proceed independently. And so Broome, convinced that he was leading his destroyers into battle against German surface forces, left the merchantmen after sending his own final signal to them; "Sorry to leave you like this. Goodbye and good luck. It looks like a bloody business."

As Broome made clear during the subsequent law suit, and also in a book he later wrote in which the story of *PQ 17* is told in detail, the "bloody business" he referred to was the battle against *Tirpitz* and *Hipper* that he imagined lay immediately ahead of him and his force of destroyers. On receipt of a signal to scatter, the ultimate in urgency, he had naturally assumed that the enemy ships might appear at any moment on the horizon. But the First Sea Lord had over-ruled his own sea admirals, had abandoned the convoy, without even checking his sources. The threat was purely imaginary, and *Tirpitz* and *Hipper* were still anchored in Trondheim on 5 July. Even worse than that, Admiralty papers since made public show that this appalling decision was no last-minute panic by an officer no longer fit to discharge his onerous duties as First Sea Lord, but a planned maneuvre that had been high among his considered options more than two weeks before *PQ 17* had ever left Iceland.

In the long days and nights that followed under constant attack, the convoy was cut to ribbons. By the end of only the second of many days at the mercy of the U-boats and the Luftwaffe, *PQ 17* had lost seventeen vessels, exactly the total number lost on all the sixteen Arctic convoys that had gone before her.

Inevitably there are those who will never forget nor forgive all that was done to them and to the men around them and under their command, and one of these is Captain H.W. Charlton, DSC, captain of the commodore ship *River Afton* (5,479 tons), torpedoed with the loss of more than twenty officers and men on 5 July. In Captain Charlton's estimate the losses suffered amounted to one hundred and fifty six lives, one hundred thousand tons of general war materials, four hundred and fifty tanks, three thousand two hundred other vehicles, and two hundred aircraft, a staggering setback to the beleaguered Russian forces with Moscow itself at that time still under threat.

From 2 July onwards the convoy was under almost constant attack by torpedo bombers, and surrounding the merchantmen were the ever-present U-boats. And then at last the executive signals began to come in from the Admiralty. First the heavy shadow force turned back, not as it happened, to face *Tirpitz* and *Hipper*, but to sail home to anchorage in Scapa Flow. Then the cruiser force under Admiral Hamilton followed them westwards, yet still the merchant captains of *PQ 17* were not unduly perturbed; these actions had been anticipated. Even the next signal "Owing to threat from enemy surface ships, convoy is to disperse and proceed to Russian ports" did not alarm them, for that too had always been a possibility – but it did puzzle them by its use of the plural 'ports'. Was the Admiralty really unaware that Murmansk was now closed, the town and the docks heavily damaged and on fire after massive German air attacks, and that the only Russian port to which they could head was Archangel? Just how 'dispersed' would be a convoy in which all the ships were making for the same destination?

Then came the fatal amendment and the order "Convoy is to scatter." Broome's reaction of tortured indecision has already been recorded. The reaction of Captain Charlton and of Commodore J.F.K. Dowding RNR aboard the *River Afton*, as they first received the signal and then saw the close destroyer escort turn about in pursuit of the cruiser squadron, was a mixture of outrage and sheer disbelief. When Broome's ship *Keppel* first flew and then lowered the "scatter" pennant the order became executive, but neither Dowding nor Charlton had expected for one moment that the merchant ships would be left with only a handful of little corvettes and armed trawlers to protect them. It was indeed, as Broome had predicted, to be a bloody business, but not for the Royal Navy and not at the hands of *Tirpitz* and *Hipper*; the blood was to be that of the Allied merchant seamen aboard the twenty-two ships that went down under attack by aircraft and submarines.

The *River Afton* herself did not escape, being struck by three torpedoes during the afternoon of 5 July. The first put the engine-room out of action and destroyed one of the two lifeboats, the second smashed the other as it was being lowered, either killing its occupants outright or spilling them into the icy water, where they died a few moments later from the cold. Only the four rafts remained now for the survivors, and as they were being launched the third torpedo struck the after-hold and sent the ship sliding stern-first to the bottom.

Chief Officer Longstaff had already lowered the master's dinghy, a tiny boat designed to hold six men at most; when Captain Charlton finally left his sinking ship, going hand over hand down a rope, the dinghy was already loaded with eleven men, and the *River Afton* still had headway of about two knots. The unstable dinghy was still attached to the ship by its painter, and as ill-luck would have it, it collided with the port lifeboat, hanging in splinters from its davit, and the men were upturned and thrown into the sea. Chief Officer Longstaff, twenty-four years old and only recently engaged to be married, drowned as he struggled in his heavy sea clothes.

Charlton clung to the upturned boat and with the help of a naval officer, Lieutenant Cook, managed to right it and clamber aboard, but the water was up to the gunwale and swirling round their waists, and the bailer was fastened to the keelson and could not be freed. On the Captain's back, however, was his briefcase containing the ship's accounts and five hundred pounds in single notes; without hesitation he sent the now useless money floating away on the surface of the Arctic Ocean and began feverishly to bale. Four frozen men were dragged aboard, one of them, a stoker, clad in a flimsy cotton vest and "with his brains like spaghetti, pouring out of a head injury. The Third officer, Harry Shaw from Hull, held him in the warmth of his armpits until, smiling peacefully, he drifted into death. We laid him in the sea, wrapped in an orange life-jacket, and we sang Abide With Me as he floated away. The Second Officer had been rescued by Chief Steward Percy

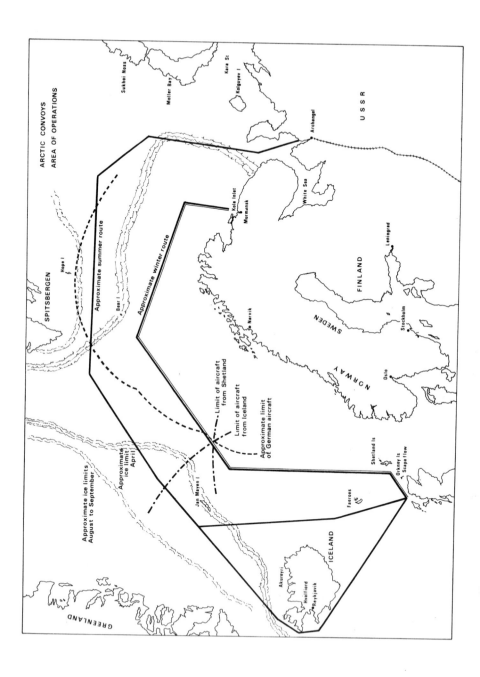

ARCTIC CONVOYS
AREA OF OPERATIONS

Grey, but poor fellow, his leg had been ripped off in the explosion, and he too died peacefully, and he too, strangely, seemed to be smiling".

But for the others, help was at hand, and very soon they were picked up by the corvette *Lotus*, which had stayed with the convoy to search for survivors. Commodore Dowding, too, had survived a lengthy immersion and completed the voyage.

There was one episode shining bright in the epic of *PQ 17*. The little armed trawler HMS *Ayrshire* was under the command of a young wartime officer, Lieutenant Leo Gradwell, a New Zealand barrister by peacetime profession, with a crew of fishermen.

Remaining with the convoy, *Ayrshire* set out to round up as many merchantmen as she could find, and she quickly established contact with two American vessels, *Ironclad* and *Troubador*, inviting them to form a miniature convoy of their own; soon afterwards, she also brought in another American ship, *Silver Sword*, and the four of them set out to seek their own salvation. From the distress signals of sinking ships Gradwell realised that on his existing course he was leading his new charges straight into the path of the U-boats, and he issued to them the practical instruction to steam straight into the ice barrier which would protect them, at least on one side, from the enemy's torpedoes; penetrating the barrier by roughly a mile, he ordered "stop engines". Then, suddenly awakened to the fact that the gunmetal grey of the ships would set them up like fairground targets against the white background of the ice-pack, he gave the inspired order that all hands, and every gallon of white paint, should be turned to the camouflage of hulls and deck-houses. *Ayrshire* and the three merchantmen under her protection merged silently with the Polar ice-cap.

After two days in concealment, when the sounds of the slaughter out to sea had ended, young Gradwell led his three dependants around the fringe of the barrier, past the north of Nova Zemlya and down through the White Sea towards Archangel. It was not to prove so easy; the ice thickened, and he was compelled to lead his little convoy south to the Matotchkin Strait, which bisected Nova Zemlya, and there the *Ironclad* ran ashore. Her captain, reckoning that simply in reaching Russia he had honoured his obligations, refused to refloat her, but he had reckoned without Gradwell's refusal to accept second best. This young officer boarded the American vessel, took over command from her captain, by use of engine, helm, and seamanship dragged her off the ice, and brought her to the settlement of Matotchkin. There he summoned up a naval escort that eventually saw *Ayrshire* and her three attendant freighters safely into port in Archangel.

Opposite: Arctic convoys area of operation

Chapter 16

IN THE BAG

For some, the war at sea ended all too early. The following notes are taken verbatim from the diary of Edwin Tiffle, POW No. 89401, Marlag, Milag Nord, and can be found in the original in the Reading Room of the Imperial War Museum in Lambeth.*

"We total 2386, 1893 of us British, from two hundred and thirteen ships sunk. 116 men and 37 lads sent home in Exchange 1943."

"Captured November 1940 by raider *Tamelayne* three days out from Australia homeward bound. Transferred after three weeks from raider to prison ship *Storrad*. Landed at Bordeaux after sixty-three days on prison ship, Feb. 5th 1941. Left Bordeaux March 12th 1941, arrived Sanbostel, Germany, March 15th and arrived at Milag Nord November 28th 1941. It is now November 25th 1944. Never been known to stay in one place so long without having to dodge the landlord."

> *"Price of Goods in Milag: November 1944*
> *Rate of Exchange: 10 Reichmarks to One Pound*

"Each prisoner receives 5 marks per month loan from British Government.

Cigarettes 100 marks per 100		£10
Pair of socks 30 marks		£3
Pair of boots 300 marks		£30
Tin of milk 60 marks		£6
6 oz sugar 20 marks		£2
1 loaf 80 marks		£8
12 oz tin of corned beef 80 marks		£8
2 oz tea 80 marks		£8

*Milag is a contraction of Marine Internientenlager. Although merchantseamen prisoners were covered by the Geneva Convention they were not P.O.W.s.

"4 oz tin of Capstan tobacco raffled in 1942 for 3000 marks – £300

"Revised prices at March 1945

100 cigarettes 500 marks		£50
Tin of milk 200 marks		£20
2 oz tea 200 marks		£20"

Extracts from letters received at Milag Nord

"Dear Daddy – I have just been to the cemetery to put some flowers on Grandad's grave. I wish it was yours. I am very busy now teaching our new daddy to speak English."

"Dear Jim – I hope you won't take this too bad, but I have decided to marry a young soldier who is doing something for his country, not like you wasting your time behind barbed wire for four years."

"Darling Joe – You may be surprised to hear after you've been away two years I have given birth to a baby boy. You may have some doubt about this, but don't worry, the doctor says it is after the same style as a delayed action bomb.
P.S. You will be glad to hear there is a Canadian officer sending you some cigarettes."

"Dear Bill – Have just discovered why you are not receiving my letters. I have been addressing them to Deutschland instead of Germany."

"Dear Jim – You will be pleased to hear that I have had the best time I have ever had since we were married. Keep your chin up dear, as I am going to the same place with the same fellow next year so I will be quite O.K."

"Dear Sam – A batch of sick men have just arrived home from Germany. They were all either badly mutilated and crippled or had a very serious illness. Hope to see you in the next batch. Love . . ."

"15th April 1945. Heavy gunfire all day from Bremen. It looks as though we are getting somewhere now. Majority of men in this camp have been prisoners for nearly five years. The boys can't come too soon . . ."

"20th April 1945. Bit of excitement last night. An exposed light from one of the barracks resulted in one of our planes diving on the camp, dropping small bombs and machine-gunning barracks, which was cut in two. Seven prisoners killed and many injured. This proved stronger than Epsom Salts to many of the lads. Hope we don't get too much of this."

"28th April 1945. Two big cars just came to camp flying White Ensign, to take over, 8 o'clock. Have just met one of our liberators, a local lad who knows me well, and he saw that I had chicken for dinner today. 11 o'clock. Great jubilation in camp. Have just hoisted Red and White Ensigns in camp square."

One of the more spectacular British seamen to fret away some of his time as a prisoner of war was Stanley Sutherland, D.S.M., who happily survived his remarkable experiences to become a master builder in his native town of Leith. Mr Sutherland makes no secret of the fact that in his younger days he might with reason have been termed a pretty hard case, and in view of his wartime adventures it was just as well for him, and for some others, that this was so.

Shortly after the outbreak of war he had signed up as cabin boy on his first ship, the *Cairn Glen*, sailing for St. John, New Brunswick, and from the first he seemed to have an extraordinary gift for leaving a vessel just before it met with disaster. After a voyage lasting two months and two days he decided to quit the *Cairn Glen*, and on its next journey home from Canada the ship foundered on the Longships. He served next as an Ordinary Seaman on the *Ruperra* (5,548 tons), suffered heavy bombardment during the evacuation from Dunkirk, and left the ship on his return to Penarth. On her very next voyage, on 19 October 1940, the *Ruperra* was torpedoed. No vessel, it seemed, could hold his interest or his loyalty for long, and he had sailed on both the *Danby* and the *Margaux* before signing up on the *Barrwhin*, bound out of Glasgow for New York; the *Barrwhin* (4,998 tons) lasted until 29 October 1942, when she too fell victim to a U-boat – but before then Stanley Sutherland had once again moved on.

This time, however, he had not carried his luck along with him and he had, moreover, come face to face with what he regarded as the essential validity of certain superstitions in relation to the sea. In May 1941, in company with his step-brother James McIntyre and with a friend from Leith, Bob Brown, he had signed up at Imperial Dock on a ship called the *Parracombe*. He had done so against the most unaccustomed and apparently irrational objections of his mother, who could offer no stronger argument than that she felt badly about the vessel and did not fancy her name. His own comment, later, is simply "Years previously my father had sailed from Leith as carpenter in a ship named the *Linmore*. She had seen this ship and 'didn't like the look of her.' My dad was washed overboard in the Bay of Fundy. Some Shetland folk have second sight."

So, it would seem, do folk from other parts. On 3 May, well on the way to Malta, a coloured seaman, John Sutherland, of Redbraes, Leith, woke up "looking the colour of death, and said 'Boys, I've been dreaming of seven white angels, and last night I dreamed a priest came and spoke to me.' Of course we all laughed at him. When our ship went down, seven out of the forecastle went down with her."

The circumstances of the *Parracombe*'s sinking were horrific, sailing as she did into one of the most densely laid minefields in the world. Stanley Sutherland again: "There was a terrific explosion, and we all hurried to the boat deck, looking for'ard. She looked all right. When I turned back to the fo'c's'le to get my Shepherd Tartan suit, my razor, and my gold tooth, some lucky lads followed me. Then there was a series of explosions that tore the bottom out of her, carrying away the bridge and killing all hands on the boat-deck. My brother Jimmie, by presence of mind, jumped into a potato-locker and closed the lid to escape flying debris. Afterwards he jumped clean over the wall with his right leg broken in three places and two toes off, but he didn't even know about this till he got ashore. I held on to a stanchion and couldn't let go till my nerves were in order again. Aft, the deck looked like a knacker's yard, debris all over the shop. By now her stern was sky-high, ready for the final plunge, and so I went feet-first over the side, and thought I would never surface again. But I did, and there was a screaming crowd hanging on to the starboard rail aft, refusing all our appeals to them to jump; they went down with the ship. Thirty officers and men we lost, and one Arab died later from exposure."

But Stanley Sutherland survived, and so did his step-brother Jimmie McIntyre, and they were about to embark upon some further adventures, straight out of *Beau Geste*. These would lead them at last, almost two years later on a day in February 1943 to Buckingham Palace, where each of them was to receive the Distinguished Service Medal from King George VI. Their story, and that of the men with whom they shared the intervening months, testifies that men of the Merchant Navy are still men to be reckoned with, even when their ship has been sunk beneath them and they themselves captured by the enemy.

After thirty hours of clinging to a raft along with two other survivors, Sutherland and McIntyre were picked up by a Vichy French seaplane and taken as captives to Bizerta and thence to Tunis, where they were marched barefoot through the streets and spat upon by jeering Italians. The prison, infested by rats and lice, left a lot to be desired, and they found no improvement when they were transferred to the Fort of Kef, in which they were to spend long months under heavy guard. No improvement, that is, till they were joined by a batch of survivors from two other ships, the *Empire Pelican* and the *Empire Defender*, the bulk of them Scotsmen like themselves, seasoned sailors with names like McDyer, McCafferty, and Hotchka McDaid, born and bred on Clydebank. McDaid's brother, setting out from Glasgow on a different ship, had been abjured by their mother to look out for him, and they had met in the same prison. "Well" said Hotchka with admirable restraint, "it's a small world." A Glaswegian of slightly different stamp who nonetheless played his part in resigning them to life in a Tunisian jail was the Reverend Dunbar, who brought them gifts from Maltese sympathisers; "we used to have a wee sermon, and it lifted up our hearts."

The padré's calming influence was not, however, quite sufficient unto the day, and eventually these turbulent Scots staged a riot in the camp and attacked their Arab guards. McDyer, McCafferty, and Sutherland himself were singled out as ringleaders and sent as punishment to a desert station, Bordj-le-Boeuf, but even this they reacted to with characteristic resilience. "It was a long run down there, and we saw a bit of the country. We told the commander of the place we were officers, and expected to be treated accordingly. Every Tuesday we had a high old time ordering stores from a nearby village, telling the storekeeper the American Consulate would pay all bills. This went on until he got a letter saying we were impostors, and then we were back on hard tack."

This did not suit them, and so they then switched to their best behaviour, and were finally rewarded by being reunited with their companions, now imprisoned in Sfax. Their captors were, to say the least of it, naif. When the Eighth Army began its big offensive, and the Italians begged for two days of grace in which to bury their dead, Sutherland and his fellow prisoners took command of their camp, annexed eighteen rifles and adequate ammunition, stole a train, and ran it to Macknassy, where they hid for two days in a phosphate mine. From there they moved on to Metloui, the first town in North Africa to fly the Free French flag, and then to Gafsa, forty miles on, where the Americans were reported to have arrived. The journey was not without incident, as Sutherland reports. "The night before we had slept for a few hours in a railway hut, after beating up a crowd of Arabs who had attacked us for our odds and ends. I smashed in one man's face with a dried bull's pizzle, which I was taking home as a souvenir." From Gafsa to Buckingham Palace his path carried him through Tebessa, Algiers, and Gibraltar, and before the war was over he had sailed again to America, West Indies, South America, Equatorial Africa, the Gold Coast, and back to New Brunswick, where his whole wartime epic had begun.

At the end of it all, sitting in a foreign cafe and suddenly hearing the radio play "Loch Lomond", he decided his seafaring days were over, signed on as a trimmer for one last voyage to Liverpool, took his discharge in Leith on 18 March 1946, and took his memories – and his Distinguished Service Medal – back with him into civilian life as a bricklayer, and later a master builder, in the Scottish town that had given him birth.

Another sailor who took less than kindly to captivity was A.H. Bird, MBE, believed to be the only member of the Merchant Navy to make a successful escape from Milag Nord. Arthur Bird, at the time of writing, is nearing completion of his own book about his wartime experiences, yet it is with his generous permission and collaboration that this chapter concludes with a brief account of his remarkable exploits as an escaper. It is remarkable not only because it is unique, but because of its ice-cool, breathtaking simplicity. Not enjoying his life as a prisoner, he simply walked away from it.

"I had been 3rd Mate aboard the *Australind*, a five thousand tonner, and my first real feeling for escape came when the raider that had captured us on 14th August 1941 was sailing so close to the Spanish coast that I felt I could almost swim ashore. Luckily commonsense prevailed, and I didn't plunge over the side to be chopped to pieces by the propeller."

There were, however, other hazards, and before reaching Germany Arthur Bird had suffered the traumatic experience of being trapped helpless aboard a vessel engaged in a running battle with ships of the Royal Navy as she passed through the Straits of Dover. She survived, and Bird and his shipmates eventually settled down to the basic problem of staying alive on meagre rations and threadbare comforts during the grim and bitterly cold winter of 1941-42.

Soon, however, thoughts of escape were once again foremost in his mind, and he greeted with enthusiasm the word that a Norwegian friend of his was engaged with some others in digging a tunnel that was already nearing the perimeter of the camp, and that he was welcome to join them in their bid for freedom. Then by sheer ill-luck one of the miners struck solid rock at a point directly beneath the patrol route of the sentries, and the sound of the blow rang out loud and clear. For Arthur Bird however the set-back was to prove a blessing, because it changed his pattern of thinking. Why depend upon ones muscles when it might be more effective to use ones wits?

"One had to be very circumspect in planning an escape or indulging in any illegal activity, for in our multi-national community the Germans had picked upon several unfortunates with relatives in occupied countries and had pressured or persuaded them into acting as informers. Nevertheless, by taking things gently, I gradually acquired the necessary compass, map, civilian clothes, and German money. What came next was harder, for I had to embark deliberately and without explanation on a course that I knew would bring down upon me, quite rightly, the scorn and contempt of my comrades."

In certain respects at least, the Geneva Convention was respected at Milag Nord, and so as an officer Arthur Bird was not obliged to engage in manual work. When he volunteered for labouring duties on a farm outside the camp, therefore, he was promptly stamped by his fellow-prisoners as a collaborator, but having realised that it was inevitable he was able to endure the stigma in silence. This, he knew, was a part of the price of freedom. He marched out daily to work on the harvest, and carefully, piece by piece, he smuggled his illicit equipment out of the camp.

"After weeks and weeks of this I ran into another hazard of the escaper – somebody else's bid went wrong, and security was tightened like a vice. There was a mass attempt at tunnelling, and suddenly the whole German apparatus was brought into play; searches in camp and close checks at the gate, and any clothing other than uniform was stamped with the letters KGF. I wondered if all my efforts would go for nothing, but luckily I had been able to hide my stuff at a neighbouring farm with an elderly owner and only one prisoner working there, who was pretty well his own boss, and it was never discovered. What I did lose, though, was time and the good weather that I'd been counting on. I had to wait for weeks more before I saw the signs that heralded a change; high, fleecy clouds in the sky, the sun shining, the earth drying out and becoming warm again. Then it was time to go."

Arthur Bird had several attributes essential to the escaper, and one of these was that he had closely calculated his chances and knew exactly what he was setting out to achieve. He knew that the guards, who after all were only soldiers, were content to see the prisoners safely on their way and headed in the right direction, rather than escorting them all the way to their place of work as regulations decreed. He also reckoned that when he failed to turn up for labouring duties, it would be several hours, perhaps even a whole day, before his farmer took the trouble to report his absence. And so he made straight for the farm where he had hidden his new identity, and within minutes, clad in civilian clothes and carrying a satchel, he was on his way across the peat bogs, bound for Harburg, on the near side of the river Elbe, or for Hamburg on the further bank. Camp gossip had reported that from both these ports ships were still plying their trade between Germany and neutral Sweden, and Harburg was only fifty miles away.

He counted upon covering the distance in forty-eight hours, and he left to intuition the decision as to whether he should travel by night or by day. At first things went wonderfully well in the sunshine, and by noon on that initial break for freedom he had made so much ground that he decided to carry straight on. That was a mistake. For his attempt to bluff his way through enemy territory involved much more than just walking. There was the moment when he stumbled upon a quarry in which Russian prisoners were working under a heavily-armed guard. There was a chance meeting in a spinney with a German officer and his girl-friend, when all that saved Arthur Bird was the fact that he had just been engaged in *Plat-Deutsch* conversation by a Polish 'voluntary worker' and so was unworthy of the officer's attention. At nightfall, having covered half the journey, he made a bed for himself in a patch of woodland, but after an hour or two he woke up in a fit of uncontrollable trembling, realising too late that the tensions of the day had taken their toll, and that he would have to pace himself more carefully.

"My stiff limbs relaxed in the morning sun, and after a bite to eat and a wash and shave in a nearby stream I set off again. It was hot that day; I was soon sweating, and my only real problem was shortage of water. When I came upon a stream and filled my bottle, I found the water was contaminated, and I had to take a chance and start begging. First I tried a nursery, and then a farmhouse with a well and a windlass in the front garden. God, but it seemed to take an age, winding up the water from that deep, deep well. Later I was hailed by a farmer passing in his cart and asked where I was going. Gruffly, but honestly, I told him in Plat-Deutsch that I was going home. I circumvented a police check-point in the approaches to Harburg, and I had a good night's sleep in the garden of a suburban villa.

"In the morning I made for the waterfront pubs, and I was heartened by meetings with Dutch and Danish seamen who told me there was still a good deal of traffic in iron ore from Sweden, though none of them could actually help me get aboard a ship. Not so encouraging were the reports of the ways in which the Gestapo were handling French stowaways. I was passing myself off as a Norwegian who had missed his ship and had been robbed, and I must have been convincing, for these fellows bought me a good meal and gave me a parcel of food to tide me over."

It was not until the sixth day after his break from Milag Nord that Arthur Bird had his real stroke of good fortune, and also the supreme test of both his nerve and his linguistic versatility. He met a group of Swedish sailors from an ore-ship and, in their own language, he told them of his true status. His gesture of trust was not misplaced, and they enthusiastically offered their help, but their ship was being watched like all the others, and it would have been courting disaster to attempt to smuggle him aboard in broad daylight. It was at this point that Arthur Bird *really* proved his courage. With his new-found friends he did precisely what any stranded sailor would do: he accompanied them to a favourite bar, 'The Golden Hind', and he passed the evening drinking beer and singing sentimental songs with a cluster of German soldiers on leave from the Eastern Front.

After dark the revellers made their way to the dock. While a few of them mounted a diversionary exercise to distract the guards at the gangway, Bird made for his assigned boarding-point abreast the fore-mast – only to find that the tide had risen and that the railing was beyond his reach. "In the darkness I found a bollard, and I stood on it apprehensively for a moment, my heavy boots slung round my neck in case I should end up in the harbour, and then I launched myself and somehow managed to scramble aboard. At that very moment, someone on the bridge lit a cigarette. Well, I reckoned he would be momentarily blinded, and I made a dash for the No. 2 hold; my friends met me in the 'tween deck and took me to a little central-heating boiler room. They were very apologetic that I'd have to sleep for the night on the bare deck, but there never was a bed so comfortable."

Next day he was given a meal and taken back to the 'tween deck, where he was tucked away beneath a mound of dunnage wood against the possibility of a last-minute search. After what seemed an age the hatches were secured and everything was dark and silent until at last came the sound he had been praying for – the *thump-thump-thump* of the diesel engine as the ship shuddered into motion and made her way to the mouth of the Elbe, where for one more agonising night she lay at anchor. Physically it was luxury, for his presence had been accepted and approved, and he had been given a sumptuous celebratory dinner before being bedded down in the forgotten comfort of a cabin – but he could not yet count himself free, for there was one more check-point ahead of him at Kiel, where the ship would once again be searched as a matter of routine.

And so, after tantalising glimpses of the scenery through the porthole, Arthur Bird disappeared once again beneath his pile of dunnage, but not before he had taken precautions to protect his benefactors should he be discovered. He had smeared dirt over his face and hands, and he had put a couple of Red Cross biscuits in his grimy satchel; if the guards should find him, he was ready to swear that he had stowed away without help from anyone. The search was duly made, and he lay beneath his woodpile listening to the jackboots tramp the deck above him: there are ways and there are ways of saying thank you.

Arthur Bird's bid for freedom had the ending it deserved. He reached Sweden in safety, but there was more, much more, to the epilogue than that. First of all, after a magnificent restaurant dinner, he was taken by his Swedish deliverers to a cinema where, ironically the film on view was Noel Coward's epic of the war at sea "In Which We Serve." Next, his appeal to the British Commercial Attaché resulted in the leader of the Swedish seamen who had befriended him being given a job with a British company that released him from his hated task of ferrying cargoes that aided the German war effort.

Most importantly, however, Arthur Bird's escape from Milag Nord brought him the reward that had inspired him to make it. In Stockholm he was reunited with his Norwegian fiancée, who had herself escaped danger-ously from her occupied homeland. Not even the movies could better *that*.

Chapter 17

THEY ALSO SERVE . . .

There are hundreds of merchant seamen who now remember with gratitude the work and the warmth of Captain P.D. Parminter, an Army officer retired after service in the First World War and his wife Germaine, irreverently and affectionately known as "Ma", who for years ran the clubs that were waiting for them in Algiers and later in Bône. They were quite a team – Parminter, the soldier who had experienced the squalor of the trenches on the Western Front, and Germaine, a vivacious Belgian who spoke four languages, could make a man smile in any one of them, and had been proprietrix of a successful hotel in Ostend.

They opened their clubs officially, of course, the husband with rank and status equivalent to Lieutenant Colonel, his wife a Lieutenant in every sense, and starting with virtually nothing they made them work. They had to. When they set up the first Merchant Navy Club in 1943 at 6 Rue de la Liberté, Algiers, just beside Barclay's Bank, the military situation in the Mediterranean and North Africa was still dangerous and uncertain, and in Algiers there were countless enemy agents speaking perfect English and only too willing to show homesick Johnnie from the boats a good time that might yield far more of value to them than to him.

The club was a place of refuge to which the sailor could come in safety and security, and although entertainment was not its primary function it did pander to convivial requirements with a bar that opened for one hour at lunch time and two of an evening. Labour was no problem; seamen just out of hospital and awaiting postings were delighted to help in return for congenial company. Discipline was no problem either to a couple as wordly-wise as the Parminters. Realising very early that while the men of the Merchant Navy could be at ease with the men of the Royal Navy, they cordially detested the army Military Police who patrolled the area, Parminter quietly arranged that policing duties at the club be taken over by the Royal Marines, and from then on there was no further trouble.

The Parminters' next step was to tackle the problem of pilfering; every day they heard tales of stocks of liquor, food, and clothing being stolen from the docks, the ships, and even from the local Services Club. They also took notice of the starvelings who hung hopefully around their own establishment each day in the guise of shoe-shine boys, and they put one and one humanely together. The scraps left over from every meal or sandwich served in the club were decently assembled and handed out to kids who were more used to being kicked away from the swill-bins, and from that moment on the stores of the Merchant Navy Club were sacrosanct - by order of the local priests.

They built up a reserve of seven hundred 'Comfort Bags' containing such items as clothing, toiletry, cigarettes, and such sweets or other little luxuries as came their way, and they found good use for them. Their greatest single 'haul' came after the sinking of the *Windsor Castle* in 1943, when they were called upon to cater for the urgent needs of two hundred survivors, one hundred and twenty of whom needed complete kitting-out, for they had lost everything they possessed. This crisis they handled with style, as befitted a smoothly-run rescue service, but their greatest triumph was more out-of-the-way - one might say bizarre - and its solution to a pressing problem carved for Germaine Parminter her eternal niche in military and diplomatic history.

With embarrassment and shy hesitance it had been brought to her notice, and hers alone, for such matters could not be discussed before men, that the local nursing volunteers were suffering all manner of discomfort, physical and psychological, because their underwear had worn out and they could find no replacement. There were difficulties, it was explained, especially in the masculine wards, because nursing duties, she would understand, involved not only close contact with the patients but movements when discretion became difficult, as when bending over to make up beds. Germaine understood perfectly, and took immediate and practical action. The signal she sent to the British Consul, and which he relayed verbatim to the Foreign Office, gave her the permission she requested to adapt suitably, with scissors and elastic, the surplus cellular drawers, sailors for the use of, that she held in stock, but what must surely endear her forever to anyone is to imagine the faces in the F.O. when that humourless band of non-combatants in Whitehall received an urgent communique from wartime North Africa headed simply and tersely "Knickers For Nurses." One could learn to love a girl like that.

As to how these two samaritans regarded the weary and bedraggled seamen passing through the area of their care, one can do no better than to quote Captain Parminter himself.

"Coming from men after what they had been through only a few hours before, and some of them for the second time, their morale was unbelievable. We found the same spirit amongst the many hundreds of Merchant Navy survivors of sunken ships we looked after during our four years with them in the Meddy."

There were others, of course, many many others, who remember what the seamen's war was all about. Mrs Mary Landergren, whose son Alfred died in the 6th Airborne Division and whose husband, a seaman, of malaria contracted in the Tropics, can even joke about it. "They used to laugh at themselves, at the picture they presented, standing there shivering on the railway platforms, decked out in whatever makeshift hand-me-downs they'd been given by the Missions, waiting for the train that would take them home to tell their families they'd been torpedoed, but they were okay. I've seen them refused a cup of tea at times like that, being told at the canteen 'Sorry, this is only for the Forces.' Mind you, if they could prove they'd been sunk, they eventually collected six quid by way of compensation."

"If he was lucky enough to sign on as donkeyman at two pounds ten a week on a weekly ship like the Methil to London run (forty-eight hours each way – if there was no fog), the first thing a man did was to buy a straw mattress, a Donkey's Breakfast, at two shillings or two and six, according to quality, and stores for the journey – half a pound of butter, bread, tea, sugar, a tin of bully beef and a pair of kippers. When he reached London, a meal in a cheap caff, then buy food for the journey back, and that was it. Unless he had a few drinks. If he had too many, his mates would throw him in his bunk and share his shift between them till he sobered up – the comradeship was tremendous, and they thought nothing of it, just 'well, what else would you do?'"

Of the countless Missions and other receiving centres for survivors scattered around the world, few better captured the seamen's imagination or held a warmer place in their affection than "The Drury Lane of Scotland", a smoky, make-shift refuge at Methil on the Firth of Forth, a little seaport of no peacetime importance that very soon became vital as an assembly point for hundreds of coastal convoys.

The location of this Mission, which functioned magnificently from the first day of the war to the last, was in itself bizarre, and lent a very special sort of intimacy to the work for which it had been created. It was huddled beneath the railway arches of Methil Station, where the coal trains plied their far from glamorous trade, but the Cedars of Lebanon could not have been more welcome or more welcoming to the weary and the wounded who came pouring through its doors, occasionally in their hundreds, for six long and terrible years. And like so many institutions of compassion, it was staffed by volunteers and supported in many of its needs by the generosity of ordinary human beings in times of danger and adversity.

Those needs, in their essence, could scarcely have been simpler, though often they were uncommonly hard to meet. Warmth, shelter, and comfort both physical and spiritual; food for the hungry, clothing for the near-naked, aid for the sick and injured, hope, security, and the restoration of faith to men who had temporarily lost all these, and often a great deal more. The messages would come in at all hours, by day or by night, maybe from the Coast Guard, perhaps from the nearby Naval station; "you have customers on the way". And Methil would come to life; missionaries, doctors, housewives, drapers would move almost without thinking into a pattern of activity that all too soon became almost routine. Fires to be lit, food to be cooked, clothing to be begged or offered; seamen to be met and transport organised at the docks, an atmosphere of home, almost of happiness, *somehow* to be conjured up. Incredibly, almost infallibly it worked, and it was this magic that gave Methil its theatrical nickname, affectionately bestowed upon it by the seamen themselves.

For not only would immediate needs be met – scalding soup or cocoa and longed-for cigarettes, extra mattresses laid out on the floor for the simply exhausted, first aid for the injured as they awaited a lift to the hospital in Kirkaldy, a blazing fire and a bundle of dry clothing for men shivering from exposure to the rigours of the North Atlantic. No, the real achievement, time after time, of the Methil Mission was in its way greater, almost, than any of these. They would provide *entertainment*, provoking participation and even laughter amongst men who only a few hours earlier had been looking death squarely in the eye. A piper or a fiddler or maybe a man with an accordion would crawl willingly from his bed, and these ragged seamen, dressed clownishly in whatever assortment of dry clothing had come their way, would find themselves actually bellowing out choruses of 'Annie Laurie' or swinging their way through an Eightsome Reel, the horror of what they had been through briefly forced from their minds by the sheer goodwill and kindness of ordinary folk who were offering a genuinely heart-felt 'thank you, and welcome – you, you at least – safely home.'

Sometimes the improvisation dreamed up by the Mission seemed positively inspired, as when the message came through one night that they were about to be inundated by no less than two hundred and sixty six survivors from eight different ships torpedoed in one of the Atlantic convoys. Many of the men, it was said, were injured and in urgent need of medical attention. This crisis, in the simple matter of accommodation, posed a problem far beyond the Mission's normal resources – but Methil would not accept mere normality as a limiting factor when help was urgently needed. One telephone call from the Mission to the Railway Superintendent was all that was required; by the time the seamen arrived, a train of coaches had been shunted in to one of the sidings above the premises, where the survivors could wait out their turn for attention, and a doctor was on hand who worked tirelessly for hour after hour while the women ladled out the soup and the incongruous clothing, and the man from the Shipping Federation paid out the money and issued the warrants that would take the men home to their families.

It was not all as easy and methodical as it sounds, of course; men died in that smoky haven because they were already hurt and damaged beyond salvation, and each person who served there has his or, more often, her especial memories – and ironically it was Methil that stood witness to the final obscenity of the Merchant Navy's war in the Atlantic.

On 7 May 1945, when the fighting in Europe had already ended, a convoy was assembled for the north-east voyage up through the Pentland Firth, but this was a convoy with a difference from all those that had gone before. On ship and on shore the lights were blazing, and at half past eight in the evening the little group of five ships set out in an atmosphere of thanksgiving that at last it was all over. Rockets and flares were ignited, messages of goodwill exchanged without restriction between merchantmen and ships of the Royal Navy, impromptu parties – and prayers – were shared by the men and women remaining on shore to celebrate the return to peace.

At eleven o'clock that night, two massive explosions were heard rolling in from the sea, and by midnight the ladies of the Methil Mission were once again at their appointed posts, on the pier-head, in the kitchen, waiting for the survivors who had been picked up by other vessels in the Firth. There were fifty four of them, from the British ship *Avondale Park* and the Norwegian *Sneland 1*, but they had left eleven shipmates behind them, two British and nine Norwegian, and another was to die before the night was out. Many more were injured, and it was morning before they were eventually taken from the refuge underneath the arches and dispatched to their respective homes. Germany's U-boat force had ended the war in Europe as it had begun it, with an unprovoked, unresisted, totally indefensible attack upon people with whom they had no war.

107

Chapter 18

SUBMARINES AND SUBMACHINE-GUNS

In 1939 Gilbert Smith took his initial step towards joining the Merchant Navy by enrolling in Wireless College, and one year later he took up his first appointment as a Radio Officer . . ." The early months were uneventful except for one Arctic Convoy, and even that was just a matter of coming to terms with nature rather than coming to grips with the enemy; we were among the lucky ones, before these journeys became *really* hellish. After that I was moved to another ship, named then simply *P.L.M. 27*, and at first it seemed I had fallen on my feet.

"She was a French vessel, you see, and I found that I had been signed up as Radio Officer and Interpreter. Well, that little distinction brought me an extra five shillings a day – a lot of money at the time – and nothing could spoil my enjoyment of *that* situation, least of all the fact that I couldn't speak one word of French. Wartime signals are pretty international, and anyway I managed to carry out my duties all right for about a year before something happened that no amount of language ability would have altered. We were torpedoed a short distance off the coast of Newfoundland."

The attack was mounted at night, and the ship simply disintegrated and sank, with not a moment to spare for the launching of lifeboats or rafts. "I went down with her just where I sat, and when I surfaced I found hatches and bits of wreckage popping up all round me, so I gathered together what I could and fashioned some sort of floating platform. This was November, and it was bitterly cold; I don't honestly know how long I paddled around, but it was long enough for me to see some of my mates alongside me eventually give up and slip under, though I learned later that others had saved themselves by striking out for the shore – we were that close. Anyway I was lucky, for I was picked up in a small boat by two fishermen who had seen the explosion and had come out hoping to help. They certainly helped me, for I don't think I could have held out much longer."

Smith was sent to the Canadian 'pool' in Halifax, where he boarded a Norwegian ship bound for England, signing off in Liverpool and joining a British vessel, the *British Chivalry*, a seven thousand ton tanker scheduled for duty as an Escort oiler. There followed months of routine activity, until, in February, 1944, she set out independently from Australia, bound for the Middle East; it was to be her last voyage, and she never reached her destination.

"Our gunners had spotted a periscope crossing our wake and had given the alarm, but that submarine could make better speed submerged than we could on the surface, and the next thing we saw was two torpedoes streaking in towards us from starboard. The helm was slammed hard over, but it was hopeless, and one of them scored a hit straight into the engine room and canted us so far down by the stern that our gun was useless. The master ordered us to abandon ship, and we had time to launch all the remaining rafts and two lifeboats, metal-built and motor powered. Of course we had casualties – six men had been killed in the explosion, and another died from his wounds a day or two later – but in a sense we seemed to have come out of it pretty well. The survivors were aboard the lifeboats, one under command of Captain Hill, the other, the one I was in, under the Chief Officer; ours was the one with a serviceable engine, and we took the skipper's boat in tow. We gathered in all the water and provisions from the rafts, and we seemed to be pretty well placed. And then the submarine surfaced."

Smith and his shipmates sat tense and watchful as the enemy tried to finish off the *British Chivalry* with shellfire and, when this proved ineffective, finally despatched her with another torpedo. They were now hailed and ordered to come alongside, where their captain was instructed to identify himself and to go aboard the enemy boat. When he did so, the remaining men in the lifeboats were ordered to proceed on their way. They saw their skipper hustled below from the conning tower and, scarcely believing in their good fortune, for they had all heard tales of Japanese atrocities, they started to move off. They had made no more than a few yards when their 'good fortune' proved false and their worst fears were realised.

"The conning tower opened again and Japanese crewmen came pouring out, but this time they were armed with submachine-guns. Our skipper was being held there, and it was obvious that he was being forced to watch what was happening. Then their gunners opened up at point-blank range, and it was hideous. Captain Hill was seen fighting and struggling to get at the Japanese sailors, but of course he was powerless. They kept it up for nearly an hour, passing and re-passing till they were satisfied they had finished us off. They'd certainly had a damn good try, and in cold blood they murdered thirteen of our men – more than twice the number they had killed in action – but quite a few of us had fooled them. Some did it by floating motionless on the water, feigning dead; others like myself played a sort of grisly hide-and-seek behind the lifeboats whenever they passed, and almost unbelievably there were no less than thirty-nine of us still alive when they finally tired of their game, closed up the conning tower hatch, and slunk away feeling no doubt well pleased with themselves.

"As soon as they had gone we hauled ourselves inboard and started to take stock of the situation. A lot of men were hurt, but only three of them very seriously, including the poor fellow who lasted only till the next day. The boats were riddled with bullet-holes, but luckily they were wonderfully well equipped with axes and other emergency gear, and soon some men were fashioning bungs while others were frantically baling, and we managed to keep them afloat; if they had been wooden instead of steel we'd all have drowned, for the firing would have splintered them to matchwood. But the engine of our boat was now completely out of action, and after attending to the wounded and checking the supplies, we sat down to work out our chances. There were thirty-nine of us, fifteen-hundred miles from the African coast, and nothing but our own rowing-power to get us there. It looked like being a long and dreary haul."

They compromised between strength and comfort at first by leaving some men on a raft that was towed behind Smith's boat, which gave the survivors some leg-room, but gave this up after about a week, when the men at the oars were becoming progressively weaker. The engine was thrown overboard, and the men were brought in from the raft, which they now cast adrift. Conditions were wretched, for the slightest movement made a man bump into his neighbour, and of course all were cramped and many covered in sores or otherwise in poor physical shape, but although tempers sometimes flared, there were enough of them to ensure that things were smoothed over, and at least they were spared perhaps the worst horror of all, of running completely out of water, although of course it was strictly rationed and in very short supply.

"Our rations were a bit laughable – a meal consisted of one-sixteenth of an ounce of pemmican, two Horlicks tablets, half a biscuit, and two ounces of water, with a piece of chocolate three times a week – but at least they kept body and soul together, and once or twice there were heavy rain squalls, when we could drink our fill. The boys behaved very well considering the conditions, and one benefit of the experience was that for once in a lifetime you could tell any damn tall tale you pleased and get away with it. We told all sorts of stories, including some real whoppers, and we regaled each other for hours with details of the meals we would have when we got ashore; there were some weird and wonderful menus worked out, I can tell you – there's no accounting for some folk's taste. We had a roster of reliable men for lookout duties, and we took turns at the oars, but we had no effective means of navigation, and really we were just drifting at large on the Indian Ocean. One day, when we'd been enduring this for about a month, we had our nearest thing to real trouble amongst some of the men, and the Chief Officer chose his own way of solving it.

That morning, and every day from then on, he led us all in a short prayer service, and even amongst the roughest customers it did wonders for morale. It may even have done more than that – who can tell? – for of course one of our principal prayers was for water, and on the very next day we were drenching and drinking in the biggest rain storm of the whole trip. The relief of this helped everyone to bear his troubles better, and spirits were high again. They were to soar right up to Heaven on the thirty-seventh day, when we sighted a ship and fired off a signal rocket. We were by this time resigned even to captivity – anything, just to be on shore again – but our luck was really running for us. She was a Lampert and Holt vessel from Liverpool bound out of India for South America, and when we were taken on to her deck we honoured a promise we had made during our daily prayers – every man-jack of us went down on his knees and gave thanks for our deliverance."

They soon learned that their rescue had been providential indeed, for instead of making westwards during their five-week ordeal, they had merely drifted south, and they were still as far from land as when they had started. But now they were safe, and ten days later the thirty-eight survivors from the *British Chivalry* were landed in Durban, where they recuperated before setting out on the long journey home. As to their Skipper, Captain Hill, Gilbert Smith learned years later that he had been made prisoner in Penang, and that his courageous struggle to prevent the brutal massacre of his defenceless men had brought him the immediate award of ninety days in solitary confinement.

Chapter 19

THE RAILWAY SHIPS

"In September 1939 I was a 'lumper', a casual dock porter, on Parkeston Quay, taking home Two Pounds Four Shillings for a forty-eight hour week at a shilling an hour less deductions. I was bitter, I don't mind admitting, after years of crawling to men I despised just so's I could be in work during the hungry thirties – and then suddenly I was a hell of a lot worse off than I'd ever been. On 3rd September I heard the announcement, and my first Air Raid Warning, and two days later I was on the dole at seventeen shillings a week. Then I had a stroke of luck, bumped into an old mate of mine called Trixie Snell, who told me where there was work for the asking.

"So I bummed up enough money for a single fare to Southampton and a bite to eat when I got there. I found a doss in the Jellicoe Hostel – there's a laugh, if you know your ranks and your Naval history – at two shillings and sixpence a night, with something to eat for another shilling. It was rough and raucous: on my first night I woke to find an enormous old shellback, dead drunk, pissing on my mattress, and I didn't dare do a thing about it, for there were far too many just like him all around me.

"But my luck was still running; on the third day there, when I was getting desperate, I saw a fellow with L.N.E.R. stamped in red letters across his seaman's sweater, and I recognised another old chum, 'Bluey' Bill Warner, told him my tale, and he bluffed me aboard the S.S. *Vienna* and shoved me in front of the Chief Engineer. The C.E. just stared at me, said 'Well, if you've trekked all the way from Harwich, I reckon you really do want work', and told my pal to get me signed on as a fireman. Then he added 'and for God's sake fix him up with a decent meal.' I still remember that Chief, for in truth by this time I was pretty thin and hungry

"Of course I couldn't really be a fireman, a stoker, not at first. There's a trick or two in firing boilers four and a half feet high, feeding a No. Ten shovel five feet back into the furnace through an aperture measuring eighteen inches across, with the coal blazing white-hot in your face every time the door opens. I learned about that later, and I learned the value of accuracy, for if you missed that door you jarred your wrists right up to the shoulder-blades and the plates burned and ripped the skin clean off your knuckles. But first they made me a trimmer, keeping three firemen supplied with enough coal to feed three twenty-ton boilers. Each boiler had four furnaces, and each furnace held half a ton; a trimmer was shovelling three tons of coal into the stokehold *every half hour*. All this in the heat and the dust and the constant rattle and hammer of the draught fans and the ringing of the shovels against the steel plating – the noise alone could drive a man almost beyond endurance."

So far as actual warfare was concerned, however, Trimmer A.J. Green and his shipmates seemed to be having things easy, with unmolested trips to Cherbourg and Le Havre escorted by destroyers that picked them up at the Needles or in Southampton Water. "Taking the BEF to France was like enjoying a holiday cruise. We drank champagne at a few pennies a magnum in Cherbourg, and would you believe it – casual visitors were being taken on conducted tours of the invincible Maginot Line. I ask you."

All too soon came the grim realities of Dunkirk, and the Railway steamers, like the holiday ships, put champagne cruising behind them and began to earn their keep. Green's crew were called together by the master, Captain Jock Pickering, and told they were needed for 'special duties' and could forget about such comforts as destroyer escorts; the *Vienna*, they were informed, would henceforth fend for herself, and if the Lewis gun that was her defensive armament *did* have a tendency to jam solid after a few rounds had been fired – well, it had worked well enough during the *last* World War, and what was good enough for their fathers . . .

Very early on in the action came one incident that remains in Green's reckoning a conspicuous act of unforced bravery. "We were in hostile waters, on our very first trip, when one of the furnace bars broke and dropped, which meant that very soon we would lose almost all pressure from one boiler, and thereby cut our speed by about a third. Well, the Fourth Engineer, Jimmy Green – no relation, I'm sorry to say – immediately volunteered to take the place of our Christmas turkey. We raked that furnace clear of burning coal and spread three soaking sacks over the blistering plates. Green put on a heavy watch overcoat, gloves, and woolly hat, wrapped a wet towel round his face, and crawled right up that damn furnace, where he replaced the broken bar – this with the other boilers blazing away full steam right alongside him. God only knows what the temperature must have been in there, but when we dragged him out he was soaking in sweat and too weak even to move. But he had done it – by sheer guts he had done it – and we pushed on safely to Cherbourg, where we picked up our cargo of three thousand French *poilus* and brought them back to Weymouth."

After coaling up the *Vienna* set out again, this time for Le Havre, and now she was to have her first taste of enemy action. "We moved in at around seven in the morning, and we could see from the fires and the pall of smoke that the town and the docks had been under heavy attack. Then suddenly we found

114

what it was all about. As we manoeuvred towards our berth we passed thirteen ships at anchor, and just as we passed them they were dived on by exactly the same number of German bombers; each aeroplane had its own target, and twelve out of these thirteen ships were hit in that one attack, though thankfully not all of them were sunk. We docked right under the harbour oil tanks, and we were probably lucky in that, for they were ablaze, and it may well have been the thick curtain of greasy smoke that saved us from getting the same treatment as our friends out there at anchor. It was no thanks to the enemy, that's certain, for the aerial attacks continued at intervals of no more than fifteen minutes throughout the whole of that day."

In between air-raids, however, the men of the *Vienna* were busily engaged in a military action of their own. Almost opposite their berth was a vast warehouse, unguarded and with its doors wide open. One visit told them it was crammed with all manner of treasures, from huge mounds of canned food to rows of gleaming, brand-new motor-cycles. It seemed a pity, to say the least, to allow this booty to fall into the hands of the enemy, now almost literally at the doorstep, and no-one has ever accused the British seaman of being lacking in resource. "We wheeled these bikes aboard, and when we found packing cases full of two-ounce tins of top-quality tobacco, we humped these cases, a hundredweight a time, as if they were feather pillows. You would never *believe* how many hiding-places there are on a ship the size of the *Vienna* – not just for two-ounce tins, but for whole packing-cases as well. Well, there seemed no sense in letting Hitler have all the Player's and Capstan, now did there?"

This happy pillaging continued throughout the day as they waited for their new cargo of retreating troops to arrive. Green and his shipmates had been puzzled by the fact that not only was this great reservoir of vital supplies unguarded, but no steps had been taken, no charges laid, no booby-traps set, for its destruction before it could fall into the hands of the rapidly advancing German army. Then, on one of their later forays, they were confronted with a possible, and unpleasant, explanation in the shape of a solitary French naval officer, who stood suddenly at the main doorway and levelled an automatic pistol at them as he ordered them back to their ship. This doubtful patriot remained on guard over the precious stores for as long as the *Vienna* stood waiting for her passengers – but he did not make any call for official reinforcement and he did not either close the warehouse or attempt to destroy its contents. Rightly or wrongly, the British seamen were unanimous in their assessment of which side would claim his loyalty when the Panzer troops rode into town.

The *Vienna* cleared Le Havre with a minimum of time to spare before the blockade closed the harbour completely. In fact she arrived in Weymouth with her keel trailing strands of wire from the defensive boom, any one of which, had it fouled her propeller, would have left her becalmed in mid-channel and at the mercy of the first aircraft or submarine to come across her in her plight. Green and his shipmates were hoping for a brief spell of shore leave – perhaps to roam the English countryside on spanking new motor-cycles – but they were immediately set to coaling ship in readiness for their next voyage, which was to start within hours and which may well, in the event, have set a long-distance steaming record for a vessel of this type.

"We were ordered to set course – zig-zag, naturally – for Brest, to pick up five thousand men of the Royal Air Force, and at once the older hands in the stokehold said 'we'll never make it; we don't carry enough fuel', but of course there was no-one of importance to listen to *them*. We made Brest all right, and laid for a few hours in the Roads, but everything was confusion; there were ships of the French Fleet bottled up there, and there were submarines all around, waiting for any of those Frenchmen who might decide to come over to the Allies. Anyway, we finally embarked our chaps without too much trouble, and then we were faced with it: we had already covered two hundred miles, much more than our usual *return* trip, and we still had two hundred more to go. We didn't feel too great about our prospects, I tell you, but next morning we tackled them.

"The order came to double stokehold watches – fourteen firemen on duty instead of seven – and the trimmers had to extract every last ounce of coal from the very corners of the bunkers. By the end of it we were actually lifting the bunker deck-plates, greedily garnering even the dust that had gathered there; I should think we trimmed coaldust dating back to the maiden voyage. Well, we made Weymouth with hardly enough fuel to fill your pipe, and we'd covered close on five hundred miles, which must surely be the longest single trip ever made by one of the old Hook coal-burners. One thing especially makes it memorable: we were actually thanked by the Chief for our extra efforts – and thanks, I tell you, didn't come easily or often from officers of the L.N.E.R."

Early in 1941 Green was transferred to another railway vessel, the *Amsterdam*, and sailed on her North-about to Aberdeen, where they arrived in the teeth of a gale so fierce that many of the heavy fittings on the ship were torn adrift. They learned there that they were to work in double harness with a sister ship, the *Archangel*, ferrying troops posted to strengthen the defences of the Orkney and Shetland Isles. Every couple of weeks these two vessels would set out with a destroyer as escort; the *Archangel* would end her run in the Orkneys while the *Amsterdam*, the larger of the two, would continue to Shetland. The sight of ruined British shipping in the supposedly impregnable Scapa Flow did nothing for morale; if the pride of the fleet could be sunk here, at anchorage in their own *sanctum santorum*, what chance had punily armed merchantmen at large on the high seas?

The myth of Scapa's invulnerability had in fact been exploded, almost literally, within six weeks of the outbreak of war. The man who planned it was Karl Dönitz, the man who carried it out Gunther Prien, and in their respective ranks and responsibilities they were to prove two of the most formidable adversaries of the Allied merchant navies throughout the most damaging and significant months of the war at sea. It was their first exercise in wartime liaison that had opened up Scapa Flow like a can of sardines and had forced the Admiralty to send the Fleet cruisers stationed there scurrying for safety to Loch Ewe on the Scottish mainland.

A few minutes after midnight on the morning of 14 October 1939 Gunther Prien, the commander of the German submarine *U-47*, followed the orders of Admiral Dönitz and stole his way, on the surface, through the maze of sunken shipping that littered Kirk Sound, the most northern of the eastern passages to the British base, gliding between the blockships and the eastern shore batteries. Although the main anchorage was almost bereft of big ships, he found hard by the northern shore a target worthy of a U-boat captain's dreams, the twenty-two thousand ton battleship *Royal Oak*, and he sank her.

The British losses were immense, twenty-four officers and eight hundred and nine crew members going down with the ship, but it is the *manner* of the sinking and the calibre of the men who planned it and carried it out that seem to justify the inclusion in this narrative of the Merchant Navy a short account of a purely military encounter between two fighting Services. It is evidence that from the very first days of the war British merchant seamen were to be the prey, the prime target, of an enemy force capable of plotting and of executing highly imaginative and dangerous attacks against even the Royal Navy's most heavily defended ships and bases.

The defences of Scapa Flow in 1939 were, admittedly, provided by the Almighty rather than by the Admiralty, but they were nonetheless formidable – yet Dönitz knew, and Prien proved, that they could be breached by a submariner of courage and resolution. That Gunther Prien possessed both these qualities was immediately proved beyond all doubt, and was to be proved again time and again during the adventurous months still remaining to him.

By 12.58 hrs on 14 October he had closed to within four thousand yards of his victim, and he fired three torpedoes, only one of which found its target, inflicting no more than slight damage near the bows of the battleship. Knowing that the alarm had been raised, and the element of surprise was gone, he nonetheless remained within range and took up a new position from which to fire his torpedo sited aft. When this second attack produced no further result, he *still* would not retreat except momentarily to re-load the forward tubes. Then, twenty long minutes after first announcing his arrival in the British anchorage, he launched a third salvo, and thirteen minutes after that, the *Royal Oak* rolled over on her side and sank. Only then, with the tides and the currents at their most dangerous, did Gunther Prien creep undetected from his single-handed attack on Scapa Flow. This was the man who, like many others of his stamp, was about to unleash his lethal talents upon the ships and men who sailed in the convoys.

It was not a submarine, however, but a German bomber that was to bring home to A.J. Green the dangers inherent to his trade. "We made a lot of these trips, and on the way home we were used to making a rendezvous with the *Archangel*. Well, one time in May '41 we reached the RV point, and there was no *Archangel* to be seen; we reckoned she'd been held up somewhere, unloading. Funny, isn't it – you never seem to think the worst, even when it's obvious. Anyway, a destroyer came alongside and told us to make straight on for Aberdeen, and it was there, next morning, we learned that she'd taken a direct hit and gone down, the first loss, I think, in the LNER fleet, though there were more to come. Well of course we went on sailing the same route, but d'you know another funny thing? For a week or two, every time we passed that RV point where she'd failed to turn up, you'd see some of the men, quite privately, looking across to the spot where she ought to have been by rights, and you knew they were thinking about our pals on the old *Archangel*."

In 1942, while refitting at North Shields, the *Amsterdam* had her defences strengthened by the installation aft of a 1914-18 vintage 12-pounder anti-aircraft gun, and Green and his colleagues were formed into teams and introduced to this and to other mysteries of naval armament, some of them so bizarre as to induce ribald merriment rather than increased confidence. "There was a steel platform, about six feet high with an elevating ramp, and fixed to this there was a rocket carrying a hundred foot coil of piano wire. The platform could revolve, and the idea was that in an aerial attack you would spin it round until you sighted your target, then you'd fire the rocket. The wire would pay out and entangle itself in the enemy's propeller – and bingo, you'd got yourself a bomber. That was the theory, but I doubt if it cost Hermann Goering many hours' sleep, and it certainly never cost him any aeroplanes. Then there was the steam-propelled missile projector, a sort of Heath Robinson trench-mortar in miniature. The mortar was a pipe attached to the steam-line from the engine room, and the missile was an ordinary hand grenade encased in something very like an old cocoa tin, open at one end, that held the lever in place after the locking-pin had been removed. When the Luftwaffe came diving down, the operator would pop a grenade into the tube and press a pedal to release a jet of steam up the pipeline; the grenade would be lobbed into the sky, and as it started to fall the air would rush into the cocoa tin, the lever would spring open, the grenade would explode, and you'd got yourself *another* bomber. That is, unless it fell back on the deck, in which case you'd probably got yourself a burial at sea. Still, we had a lot of fun with that contraption, for we used to while away the time, now and again, by aiming it at other ships near by – only for ammunition we used potatoes from the galley, not grenades. Maybe these brainchildren made a lot of money for their inventors – I wouldn't know – but to the fellows who had to use them they were the biggest joke of the war."

For the crew of the *Amsterdam*, however, armament became a much more serious matter in the middle of 1943, when in a great bustle of activity they found the ship being fitted with weapons that gave a clear promise or warning of dangerous operations ahead. In addition to a brand-new naval 4-inch anti-aircraft gun installed aft she was equipped with four Oerlikon cannon amidships, and to the ship's complement was added a team of naval D.E.M.S. (Defensively Equipped Merchant Ships) gunners. Administratively, too, there was a foretaste of things to come, for the civilian crew were assembled in No.3 hold to be told by the master and by an official from the Ministry of Transport that they were being asked to sign new Articles known as Special Operations For The Liberation Of Europe, which grandiose and purposeful title signified in effect that in future, should their ship be out of commission, they could be immediately assigned to another vessel, with the humane proviso that if their availability was the result of their ship having been sunk, they would be entitled to Survivors' Leave. "At first some of the men weren't too happy about this, but then one old hand said gruffly 'Look – we'll all sail anyway', and it was so obviously true that everyone just signed up without any fuss or argument."

Their new assignment carried them down the east coast and through "E-boat Alley", a very respected stretch of water, a forest of masts reaching up heartbreakingly through the surface, to Weymouth, where the *Amsterdam* was re-designated L.S.I. (Landing Ship Infantry) and where she took aboard an additional complement of one hundred and fifty American Rangers and half a dozen L.C.A.s (Landing Craft Assault), which were slung from davits on the boat deck. Their future was now clear beyond all doubt, but first there came weeks of training, a prolonged exercise in inter-Service and indeed international collaboration.

"We would sail maybe fifty miles down the coast and then launch the LCAs, each of them manned by two naval ratings, who would bring the boats back to us as soon as a landing had been effected. The Rangers, kitted out with grappling irons, ropes, and all the gear needed for coastal invasion, would be left to scale the cliffs and eventually to find their own way back to base without detection by 'defending' forces who might well have been alerted to their arrival. And believe me, we landed these boys in some very wild and inhospitable places. This training went on for a long long time, and we got to know something about how the other half lives.

"There was no ship's food for these lads; they had their own cooks and their own rations, with chicken and ice-cream and all sorts of delicacies forgotten in England. Then we'd see them with their big cigars, gambling hundreds of dollars in a single game of poker, more than we would earn in months – but do you know, even then there was no personal resentment, though of course we sometimes grumbled as we thought of the pittance we were being paid. I think the goodwill came simply because they were such a grand bunch of fellows, tough and well trained, ready for anything, and I reckon all but the daftest among us knew very well that for a lot of them it would be the last fling they would ever know, and that each one of them had volunteered for the danger he would so soon be wading in to meet. By early 1944 we were all conscious of a tremendous upsurge in spirits and expectations; we knew deep down that at last we were winning, and we knew too that these young Americans who were sharing our ship would be in the very forefront of the attack when it came – and they were: I often wonder how many of them ever saw the United States again."

That question cannot be answered here, but this much is known; of those six LCAs laden with US Rangers, only one returned to the *Amsterdam*, and the sea was so bad at the moment of the assault that two of them sank as soon as they had cleared the parent ship, five miles off the Normandy beaches. For the seamen left aboard the railway ship, A.J. Green among them, there followed fifteen hours of frustration as ringside spectators of the greatest seaborne operation in history, waiting, because they had to wait, to find out whether the landing had succeeded or whether their next orders would be to close the shore in an action not of invasion, but of rescue and retreat.

"Of course we didn't know what to expect, and in a way it was almost funny at first, seeing stokers go down below wearing tin hats and life-jackets, instead of just their usual singlet, slacks, and sweat rag. But pretty soon we were right on the borders of a battle such as no-one, anywhere, had ever seen before. First there was this incredible aerial blanket of fighter-bombers saturating the beaches and the countryside beyond; the sky was full of them, bombing and straffing – and then there was the sight of this battleship, a huge, graceful monster, making run after run to bombard the shore defences. She would speed straight in for the shore and then, with helm hard over, she would turn at right-angles and open up with a broadside of 14-inch shells, tons and tons of high explosive hurtling in to blast the land and soften up the defences in preparation for the main assault. No sooner had the battleship loosed off a salvo than she would turn seawards, straighten up, and go through the whole business again from the opposite side; the thundering noise and the activity all around and above you – it was just unbelievable. And yet, as a spectacle, it was almost overshadowed by what lay ahead of us when finally we got the order to sail for home.

"Not even the film-makers, nearly forty years later and with all their marvellous modern technology, succeeded in recapturing on the screen the sight that met our eyes as we made our way back across the Channel. Wherever you looked, on all sides and right to the horizon, there were ships – big ships, packets, tugs and destroyers, fishing boats, tankers, landing-craft and MTBs, thousands of them, rank after rank, wave following wave, the greatest invasion the world had ever seen. Twenty miles out men were working like demons on Pluto, the miracle that made it all feasible; crippled craft were being towed towards *France*, with no thoughts of limping for home before they'd discharged their cargo of men or munitions; it was the most awe-inspiring sight any one of us had ever experienced – and *Amsterdam*, the old Hook to Harwich ferryboat, was right there in the middle of it, playing her part like the rest."

Nor was the *Amsterdam*'s part in the war yet over, for with her service in the invasion successfully completed she was scheduled yet again for re-fitting and a change of duties. This time her prized armament was taken away from her and replaced with bunks and wards and a fully-equipped operating theatre, in readiness for her new assignment as a hospital ship. In place of American troops she now carried doctors, nursing sisters, and medical orderlies, and instead of her protective colouring of crab-meat grey she was now painted overall in shimmering white, with huge red crosses on her sides and a broad band of emerald green encircling her from stem to stern. And to fit her for her new requirements, the watertight bulkheads were breached to allow more room and greater freedom of movement below decks; that this would also reduce her buoyancy should things go amiss did not pass unnoticed by the crew, and there was one other condition of their new role that they greeted with unashamed misgivings. For their next voyage into the war zone they were ordered to sail at night-time with all lights ablaze. It is not hard to imagine the effect of this well-meant instruction upon men who for years had lived behind darkened ports, believing that even to light a cigarette in mid-Atlantic was to invite destruction at the hands of a prowling U-boat. "We didn't like it, and I'll not pretend we did. We didn't trust the magic of the Red Cross, and we didn't trust the Germans – and by God, we were right on both counts."

The *Amsterdam* made two trips to the beach-heads and back, carrying home hundreds of wounded young men, manhandling them aboard in makeshift slings and stretchers from the flat-bottomed craft that had brought them off-shore. These wounded men had come to them straight from the field dressing stations and were unkempt, unwashed, and as yet with little more than first aid attention to ease their pain. "When it came to loading, the whole crew turned out to lend a hand, on or off watch – it was the very least we could do to help these lads and try to bring them some tiny bit of comfort. It was a soul-destroying job, but it didn't last for long.

"On our third trip I had the graveyard watch, 12-4 a.m., while we were lying off the beach-head with five hundred stretcher cases and a load of walking wounded, waiting to sail for home in the morning. It was an unbearably hot and clammy night, and when I came off duty I broke my usual seagoing rules by stripping right off and having a shower. I lay down and dozed off, and my awakening was horrific; I was vaguely conscious of a tremendous crash, but found I was already under water and unable to stop myself swallowing – the concussion must have stunned my lungs, and I just could not force the water out. I was struggling through almost solid debris, and my chest was on fire and ready to burst, when suddenly the weirdest thing happened to me. I became conscious of a brilliant light directly above, and in that circle of light I saw quite clearly a picture of my wife and my daughter looking down at me. I was aware of thinking 'this is the end', and I was astonished at how calmly I was taking it, still choking, but quite cool and resigned to accepting it. At that very moment I finally broke through to the surface.

"I have no idea even now as to how I'd managed it, but I was some way clear of the ship, and I could see she was finished, with a great ragged tear almost cutting her in half. Still, though she was listing badly, she was still floating, and I swam back to her and started to clamber aboard. There were no natural handholds, of course, and the only way I could get aboard was to clamber up the jagged edges where she'd been ripped. I was tearing myself to pieces in the process when suddenly I came to my senses and realised I was climbing up the side to which she was sinking, but I was too late to change and start again, and somehow I just managed to haul my upper body inboard as she started to settle. Then a crazy scramble up the angled deck, past broken davits, twisted wreckage, and the body of a soldier who had been cut clean in half. Crazy? Another soldier crawled past me, leaving his pyjama trousers behind him – well would you believe it, in that second I became suddenly conscious of the fact that I was naked as the day I was born, and bleeding like a pig, on a sinking ship, I struggled into that man's discarded pants to cover my nudity. My God, the things you do – but then, there's not much sense in any of it, is there?"

In the sinking of the *Amsterdam*, a hospital ship clearly marked, hundreds of wounded soldiers drowned in their bunks and stretchers, and it nearly spelled the end for A.J. Green. After weeks in hospital he returned home stone deaf, afraid for weeks to venture out alone, riddled with guilt and unwilling to face the dependants of friends who had not survived – a common unhappiness, this last, amongst survivors of his age and generation, and one that may ease, but time may never entirely erase. After his partial recuperation the L.N.E.R. offered Mr Green a job scraping boilers: he worked at it till he had mustered up enough money to leave the sea for ever, nearly forty years ago.

Chapter 20

THE LIBERTY SHIPS

The contribution of the United States to the Allies' effort in the war at sea, both before and after Pearl Harbor, could scarcely be over-estimated. Without it Britain simply would not have survived, and nowhere is this more graphically illustrated than in the story of the Liberty Ships, prefabricated to a standard basic pattern and churned out with astonishing rapidity to make good the disastrous losses to the U-boats during the early years of the war.

The miracle of the Liberty Ships is instantly linked with the name of Henry Kaiser, an American engineer whose understanding of the principles of prefabrication and mass-production made the whole project viable. His professional record was impressive, for he had played an important part in the construction of the San Francisco Bridge, as well as the Hoover, Coulee, and Shasta Dams, and he directed the Permanente Cement Co. of Richmond, California, which was to mastermind the building of the new ships. He based the whole programme on prefabrication, and his was the imagination and daring that dispersed the contracts for part-construction all over the United States, including cities and factories far from the sea. His initial contract was to build sixty ships, and from that beginning the project blossomed. Kaiser's achievement was in *production*, and did not include the original conception and design of the Liberty Ship. That distinction belongs to the design staff of the Joseph L. Thompson shipyard of North Sands, Sunderland, England, where the first of the breed was constructed as early as 1935, to the order of Hall Bros., shipowners, of Newcastle-on-Tyne.

During the depressed years of the nineteen thirties the Thompson company had been far-sighted enough to modernise their shipyard and to set their design staff to the planning of a standardised cargo vessel of the future. What the staff came up with was the prototype *Embassage*, nine thousand three hundred tons, with a raked stem and a rounded stern, a coal-burner powered by three North-East Marine triple-expansion engines, and it was upon the *Embassage* and twenty-four others like her, built in the thirties, that the design of the wartime ships was to be based. The very first of them was built in Britain, commissioned by the British Government, and sailed in early 1941 under the management of R. Chapman and Co. of Newcastle. Her name was *Empire Liberty*, and it is from her that all the others derived their distinctive classification.

They were built in Britain, Canada, and America, and in each case the ship's name gives the answer as to its place of origin. In some instances the name tells a little more than that, for the Canadians drew a fine and proud distinction between those of their vessels crewed by Canadians and those that sailed under the plain Red Duster. The names of the former carried the suffix 'Park', whilst those under British command bore the prefix 'Fort'. Both categories performed magnificently, carrying vital cargoes anywhere from the Arctic to the Azores. American-built ships generally carried either the prefix 'Ocean' or the suffix 'Liberty', although some crewed by Americans would be named after a citizen of distinction. The Liberty Ships constructed in Britain bore the prefix 'Empire'.

There were other distinctions, too, between the American Liberties and the British or Canadian *Empires*, *Forts*, or *Parks*. The American ships had a housing around the funnel in which were accommodated the officers and crew and the navigating bridge, and they were fuelled by oil instead of coal. The British and Canadian vessels did things differently, with a house abaft the funnel quartering the engineers, Petty Officers, and catering staff, while the master and the deck officers, and the bridge, were stationed for'ard. The outline of the ships was different, but the basic design was identical, as was the armament, consisting usually of 4-inch low angle guns and 12 pounder anti-aircraft weapons as well as Oerlikons, Bofors, cable and parachute projectors and other contraptions designed to menace enemy aircraft with hand grenades or coils of wire. A few, including those built in Britain, also carried an altogether more serious weapon – a catapult-launched Hurricane fighter which could be launched only once, to give some air defence against marauders such as shore-based Fw 200 Condors. His mission completed, the pilot had only two unenviable choices – to bale out or to ditch his aircraft, hoping in either case that he would be plucked from the sea by his parent ship.

The belt-feed production of the Liberty Ships was a spectacular example of international co-operation, and it was no more than fitting that Henry Kaiser's liaison officer, appointed as head of Britain's negotiating team, should be Cyril Thompson, son of Major R.N. Thompson, chairman of the company that had given birth to the whole idea. It was an inspired, if obvious, appointment, and in several quite different ways Cyril Thompson (later made a C.B.E.) proved his worth. He pioneered the extension of the production programme to include Canadian shipyards and it was he who, when the ship on which he was returning to England was torpedoed on 14 December 1940, rallied the survivors and pulled his weight on the lifeboat's oars. Later, tired of his wartime occupation as an administrator, he qualified to fly as a member of an operational aircrew in Bomber Command.

Chapter 21

TED WADSWORTH FINDS HIS SEA-LEG

Ted Wadsworth is a remarkable character – in 1930, as a lad of fifteen, he had one leg ripped off by a rogue hawser during his first voyage to Kobe, Japan, yet within two years, in a time when fully-trained, able-bodied sailors were ten a penny and scrabbling for jobs, he forced his way back into acceptance as a member of the Merchant Navy, in which he was to serve, all told, for forty-one years.

The struggle had not been an easy one; amongst other tests, he had scaled forty-foot ladders in his bid to prove he was as good as the next fellow, and better than some. His self-belief was vindicated handsomely in the years to come, when he not only sailed throughout the war, sunk by both submarine and aircraft, pulling his weight in actions from Anzio to the Arctic, but on one memorable occasion actually made use of his disability to shame, or to inspire, a shipmate into improbable survival.

In October 1940 he was aboard the *Sandsend*, a three and a half thousand tonner carrying a load of anthracite between Hull and Nova Scotia when, on the 17th, the convoy was attacked by a submarine after moving north-about around the Scottish coast. "It was a raw, wet, dirty night and all we could see, standing watch, was white horses in the darkness, until suddenly there was this tremendous flash, and then another one, and we knew some poor devils had bought it. Well, there was nothing we could do or were even allowed to do; I don't even know the names of the ships that went down that night, and in a way I'm glad, for even if there were any survivors I doubt if we'd have been able to spot them, let alone to save them, the conditions were so bad. So we just steamed on, wondering if it would be our turn next."

It was. On the morning of the 18 October the U-boat struck again, and this time her victim was the *Sandsend*. "I was still on watch – yes, been on it all night – when there was this awful explosion, and I knew right away we were done for. Smoke was billowing out of the engine room, where we'd taken the hit, and the funnel just sort of tottered and then fell over on its side. The deck was a shambles, and only the starboard lifeboat was still there. One look down into the engine room was enough to tell us there could be no-one left alive down there; the ship was starting to settle, with a great hole torn in her port side, and so we lowered away."

The survivors had succeeded in pulling the life-boat clear when one of them shouted "where's Sparky?", and the men at the oars, Ted Wadsworth one of them, stopped rowing and gazed back at the sinking ship. Through the smoke they could just make out the figure of the Wireless Officer standing by the bow, which was by now high out of the water, and the master, Captain Armstrong, shouted to the young man to run further aft and then to jump for it, which he did. Wadsworth tells what happened next.

"We started puling in towards him, as close as we dared, for the *Sandsend* was going down fast and we might all have been sucked down with her, and we shouted to the lad to swim as hard as he could. We could see he was wearing his life-jacket, and he was afloat all right, but he wasn't making any movement, and of course we thought he might be wounded or unconscious. Well, I dropped my oar and jumped over the side. I heard Captain Armstrong calling to me to sit down, but there wasn't anything heroic about it – I just couldn't sit there and watch that lad drown within sight of us. I dog-paddled my way over to him and could see he was conscious although he had a dazed sort of look about him, and his head was flopping about in the waves. I spluttered a couple of gallons of salt water out of my mouth and said to him 'are you all right?'. He just nodded and did nothing else, so I said 'Look, son, if I can get here and back with one bloody leg full of water, I reckon you can manage a one-way trip, so start paddling if you can't swim.' And do you know, it worked; with me hanging on to him we somehow made our way back to the boat, and a dozen hands hauled us inboard, half-dead. Funny, the things you do without really thinking, isn't it?"

It is indeed. The pleasing tail-piece to this incident is that 'Sparky's' tendency to hesitate proved to be a distinctly two-sided coin. Certainly his sudden violent immersion had stunned him momentarily into irresolution – but the reason for his *being* in the water, the reason for his not having boarded the life-boat with his shipmates, was that he had remained too long at his post, sending out the distress signals that might help to ensure that they would all be saved. "What a lad" says Ted Wadsworth. "I'm proud to have been able to give him a hand."

The drama of the *Sandsend's* sinking was not yet over, and what followed gives an interesting glimpse into the mind of one, at least, of Dönitz's U-boat captains at a time when their star was still very much in its ascendancy. "There was a damn great *whoosh*, and up comes the submarine, not fifty yards away from us; the conning tower opens, and we think 'Christ, what comes now?' Then in perfect English, far better than I can speak, he asks if we have any wounded who need attention; if so, he'll have them treated and returned. No response. Well, are we short of water, or cigarettes? Not a word. Will our captain come aboard? 'He went down with the ship.' A damn lie; Captain

Armstrong was sitting there with us, but of course he wasn't going to give himself up as a prisoner. Then this U-boat commander says – would you believe it? – 'Stay as close to this position as you can. There is not much tide, you have sent your signals, and you are bound to be rescued soon. Good luck. I am sorry to have done this to your ship and to your men, but we are at war; you will see your own country before I ever see mine.' He was most probably right, the way things went – but I mean, would you *believe* it, in 1940, in the middle of the Atlantic?"

The German commander was proved right on at least one count. In the early evening of the sinking, the *Sandsend*'s survivors saw smoke on the horizon and resigned themselves to captivity, at the best; clearly, a mopping-up operation had been mounted. But the ship bearing down upon them was the British corvette *Ibiscus*, which circled them carefully before ordering them to throw everything superfluous out of the lifeboat as quickly as possible and come alongside. "Well we did, as you may imagine, and we were hauled aboard, given hot drinks and the cigarettes we were longing for but had refused from the U-boat because it simply didn't seem right when they'd just sunk us and killed our mates, and we were given dry clothes or blankets and shovelled into bed. It wasn't till later we discovered that the bunks we'd been lying in so thankfully had been made vacant for us by the off-duty watch – we knew then that sailors are sailors and it doesn't matter a damn whether you're Royal Navy or Mercantile Marine. These blue-jackets, without even telling us, bedded down on the deck.

"We found out one other thing, from the corvette's captain. The only reason they had been able to find us and to pick us up so quickly was they had been given our location by *one* signal, and one only – the very last one that Sparky had sent."

U-boat crewmen display their trophies, wreckage and a flag from a US freighter. The entry of America into the war brought a new 'happy-time'

Hoisting a 6-inch gun aboard a merchant ship. Such improvisation brought a measure of protection against surface raiders

First-World War vintage machine-guns on a crude anti-aircraft mount pitched against the might of the Luftwaffe on an Arctic convoy

Seen from a U-boat, the fiery end of a torpedoed tanker

Sherman tanks for the embattled Red Army arrive safely at Murmansk, 1942

*Right: Contrast in styles – heavy lift equipment at
Murmansk and a horse and cart – each in their own way
vital components in maintaining the flow of supplies*

The battered Ocean Freedom, *survivor of Convoy PQ17, limps into Murmansk*

British and Soviet seamen in Murmansk

Survivors of a torpedoed merchant vessel are hauled in from an upturned lifeboat. Survival time in Arctic waters was numbered in minutes

Return to Murmansk. The author at the cemetery where men of the Merchant Navy and others of Britain's services who gave their lives on the Arctic convoys are buried

Chapter 22

THE D.E.M.S. GUNNER

In 1942 Roy Trowsdale, like many another eager youngster, enlisted in the Royal Navy, full of dreams of mighty battleships, sleek destroyers, and glory to be won in the greatest fighting Service in the world. Fourteen weeks later, after basic and gunnery training, he was posted for duty on his first ship, the *Tintern Abbey*, a shop-soiled, dismal, two and a half-thousand ton coaster with a top speed of fourteen straining knots.

On the *Tintern Abbey* and four other similar vessels he sailed some sixty-thousand miles during the next four years, and it was not until the war had ended that he first stepped aboard a ship of the Royal Navy. In the beginning he was perhaps a little bitter, for apart from disillusion he suffered initially from chronic sea-sickness, his only previous experience of the ocean having been paddling on the beach at Skegness. In those early days, had there been a way out, he would have taken it without hesitation. But in wartime there was no way out. He was a D.E.M.S. gunner, seconded for duty in the protection of the Merchant Navy, and after cursing his luck he settled down to the business of learning and later appreciating his trade. This is how he now sums up his wartime experience.

"Hitler, there is no doubt, was an evil man, but I must confess that but for him I wouldn't have seen the sights I have seen, travelled as I have travelled, been scared as I have been scared, laughed as I have laughed, and ended up a better man, I think, than I would have been without him. Indirectly I have him to thank too for a wonderful wife, daughter, and grandchildren, so all in all I didn't do too bad. But behind all that, a part of all that - I learned most of what I know because of that chance, unpopular posting that introduced me to the Merchant Navy, the *real* men of the sea."

Roy Trowsdale's admiration of the merchant seamen he served with is unbounded and sincere, and it spans the whole length of his wartime experience. "The skipper on my first trip was the legendary Spud Jones, who had made his name during the Spanish Civil War, running cargoes of potatoes through the blockade. Always sporting his trilby hat, clearly loving the pipe that was never out of his mouth, he was ice-cool even at the worst of times, and he always had time for a friendly, encouraging word – he really gave you the confidence you needed so badly. First time he spoke to me I was on watch, and all he said was 'first trip?' – but the way he said it, and the half-smile on his lips, just warmed me through and through."

It is through quick glimpses like this, rather than through memories of great events, that Roy Trowsdale, the RN 'outsider', adds to the picture of the Merchant Navy at war. "The awful sea-sickness, the rolling of the ship, the smell all the time of swede and Irish tinned butter from the galley, the time I got stuck in an inboard porthole after locking myself in the heads – no funny situation when there may be a torpedo coming any minute – and had to be helped free by the crew; all this was pretty awful. But gradually I started to watch the old hands at work, never fussing, just getting on with the job in hand, and I started to learn. Then one day – this was in the Arctic – I was standing watch and it was piping strong. We had the canvas cheater up to protect us, for that wind, I tell you, had *ice* in it, and suddenly there was this seaman, head up, peering over the top of the screen and never batting an eye. He was lean and tanned and he looked about fifty, an old man to me at that time. I thought 'if you can do it, Grandad, so can I', and I stuck my head up over the cheater. Well, the blast took my breath away, my eyes were pouring, and I ducked down again damn quick; I just couldn't stand it, not even for a minute. I looked at this fella, standing there quite still and silent, and I thought 'what are you chaps made of – bloody iron'?"

He saw evidence, too, of the strains that sea-going can impose, and he saw how different men react. There was the occasion when, on watch in equatorial waters, he was startled by a sudden bout of manic yelling that he traced to another D.E.M.S. gunner, off duty and leaning over the rail. "What the hell was all that about?" demanded Trowsdale. "Oh, I just felt like it" responded his friend, and went on with his otherwise silent contemplation of the ocean.

More serious was the time when, after some shuttle-service between Gibraltar and the Spanish port of Almeria, his ship, allegedly en route for UK, was closed by a British MTB and ordered to return to the Rock. The skipper ignored the order, and ignored its repetition even after a warning shot had been put across his bow. When he then ordered the D.E.M.S. gunners to open fire on the MTB, they naturally refused, and the Captain was physically overpowered by the First Mate, who steered the vessel back to Gibraltar, where the overstrained skipper was summarily relieved of his command.

The sudden transition from peace to war affected the skippers no less than it did the seamen under their command. Not all, but many of these men had been quietly plying their trade around the coasts or the oceans, 'commanders' solely because of their experience in handling small steamers or even barges or tugs, and no part of their training or their temperament had prepared them to contend with bombs and torpedoes, nor to fit them for the task of directing men as untried as themselves in the face of enemy action. In addition to the new danger they had the unasked for responsibility for other men's lives in totally unfamiliar circumstances, and it is scarcely surprising that some of them should have failed to measure up. A strip of gold braid does not necessarily carry with it the capacity for leadership under fire. Yet Para Handy was more memorable in his way than Captain Johnnie Walker.

Certainly the witnessing of one man's temporary weakness is outweighed in Roy Trowsdale's mind by the memories of the other men he served with, of their calmness under attack and their determination to "just get on with the job". It would be hard to better his final tribute as a shipmate from another Service.

"I was proud of the Royal Navy, and I respected the uniform that I wore, but you can believe me when I say that I would have traded both for the honour of wearing that little silver badge with the letters M.N."

Chapter 23

LONG DAYS AND LONG NIGHTS

There were some merchant seamen to whom Russia meant not simply voyaging to the Arctic, but actually living there for many months on end. One of these was Second Officer Maurice Irvin, MBE, of the *Empire Elgar*, a vessel of two and a half-thousand tons specially fitted with heavy cranes for lifting tanks, and his recollections give an insight into life in the Soviet Union during the tense and dangerous years of 1942 and 1943.

He had sailed in *PQ 16*, a convoy of thirty-five merchant ships, of which seven had been lost, and he had survived one particularly gruelling battle remembered by the men who went through it as 'Bloody Wednesday'. He had been awarded the MBE for his conduct and for an inspired piece of navigation during the later stages of the voyage, when the convoy had been split in two and his ship, the *Empire Elgar*, ordered to lead one of the groups on an uncharted run for Archangel instead of their intended destination, Murmansk.

In Iceland, waiting for the convoy to set out, he had confided to his opposite number on another vessel, the *Empire Purcell*, that he was somewhat less than entranced by the prospect of many months of heavy-lift duties in some God-forsaken port in the Arctic, and had been astonished when his friend expressed not commiseration, but open envy. He, it seemed, was experiencing domestic difficulties of such severity that he would welcome almost any alternative to the necessity of returning home. The man was serious, and next day he and Irvin applied formally for an exchange of postings. Since they had identical qualifications the request was given sympathetic consideration, and was in fact turned down only because of the complications involved in amending Articles while their ships were in foreign waters. It is not hard to imagine Maurice Irvin's feelings only a few days later when, on Bloody Wednesday, he saw the *Empire Purcell*, alongside him, hit by an air-launched torpedo. She was loaded with munitions and disappeared in a gigantic flash, leaving nothing behind her but scraps of wreckage and a few bodies floating in the icy water. Another of his more poignant memories dates back to his first few weeks in Russia, when he and his shipmates, tied up in harbour, saw some of the pitiful remnants of *PQ 17* come limping in. Before sailing, the *Empire Elgar* had been presented, for obvious reasons, with a gramophone recording of Pomp and Circumstance, and again it requires no very vivid imagination to visualise the reactions of the survivors as they steamed into port to the strains of Land of Hope and Glory.

In the weeks and months that followed, Maurice Irvin had experiences that set him apart from most of his brother officers in the Merchant Navy. He was to be engaged in the duties not so much of a sailor as of an engineer, supervising the landing of tanks weighing up to thirty-eight tons onto wooden jetties; he was to spend most of these months anchored against the harbour wall of ports under constant attack from the air; he was to discharge his duties in a foreign country, instructing foreign nationals in complex and sometimes dangerous skills, in a language of which he did not, at the outset, speak one single word. The drawbacks of this linguistic limitation made themselves immediately apparent when a Russian official, ignoring Irvin's signs of warning and hand-expressed offer of help, insisted on taking over control of the winch, and dropped the very first tank landed from the *Empire Elgar* clean through the timbers of the quay constructed especially to receive it. Such misunderstandings – and the jetty – were swiftly put to rights, and disembarkation proceeded apace.

Some seamen, including Irvin himself, a modest man, might say he had it lucky: he was alive, he was an officer, and his time spent in Murmansk, Archangel, Molotovsk, and Bakaritsa included moments enjoyable, and even comfortable moments, as well as the time on the convoys. But the good times were few and far between and they were simple in their essence. He shared shamelessly in the liquid delight of his crew-members in the cargo-hold who had broached a case of malt whisky that some idiot had dispatched unmarked; he traded nutty, the seaman's sweetmeat, for vodka or omelettes or even music from the band in the few shore-establishments, like the Arctic or the International Club, that offered momentary respite from the daily routine of work and bombs.

As in every theatre of war, barter was the order of the day, with cigarettes and chocolate the main items of currency. With the official exchange rate at forty-eight roubles to the pound sterling, a packet of twenty cigarettes would fetch forty roubles; in their turn Irvin and his shipmates would spend thirty roubles on a quarter-litre of vodka or sixty-eight on a bottle of muscatel wine. Children roamed the wooden streets with their pockets crammed with money, eager always for a deal. It was not a matter of taking advantage of an impoverished people, but simply of striking a bargain acceptable to both parties, and it helped to make tolerable long weeks and months in an inhospitable environment. And it *was* inhospitable. The Russians, with millions of their people already dead or captured and the country's very existence in daily peril, were in no mood for light-hearted fraternisation, which indeed was punishable by instant incarceration in a labour camp.

Fraternisation could, however, be engineered – within very strict limits. At such social centres as the International Club in Archangel, which Irvin and his mates swiftly adopted as their off-duty headquarters – there were dances, with specially vetted and chaperoned girls in attendance as partners. With one of these girls, an attractive blonde named Tanya, Maurice Irvin struck up a friendship that was to last for many months, but he had to come to terms with the fact that outside the dance hall, if they met, he would and could be greeted by no more than the cursory civility of an acquaintances' chance encounter. And so, despite the fact that they frequently travelled on the same ferry that took her across the river to her home and him to the ship's berth at Bakaritsa, a few miles from Archangel, their undoubted affection for each other never progressed beyond an occasional furtive squeeze of hands when they were sure no-one was watching them. The Merchant Navy men on the Arctic run faced many dangers, but not those of their colleagues on the convoys to Malta and the Middle East.

Another cause of frustration and discontent was brought to the surface when a contingent of Royal Air Force personnel was billeted for a time at the "Interclub", where they held quite a number of parties. It was not the airmen, nor their parties, that irked the men of the Merchant Navy; they got along well with the former and were regularly and cordially invited to join in the latter. The resentment was caused by the glaring discrepancies in the treatment meted out by the British government. Not only were the airmen supplied with NAAFI stores and given a regular and generous ration of cigarettes, beer, and chocolate – they were actually awarded an extra expenses allotment from which to pay for these luxuries. As for the seamen, the fellows who had brought the stores to Russia in the first place – well, they were mere civilians, and as such, entitled to nothing. It was so outrageously unfair that they were moved to repeated official protest, and finally the rules were grudgingly amended to allow them to purchase a ration of cigarettes and chocolate, with a half-promise of a beer ration "when supplies improved." The next supplies arrived on Convoy *PQ 17*.

Security regulations were another thorn in the side of all British personnel stationed in Russia. On the docks passes would be inspected time after time by sentries. Yet even this side of Arctic life had its funny moments. Maurice Irvin, calling one evening on his friend Lieutenant Sydney Newman of the *Alynbank*, ran the gauntlet of sentries only to be greeted with consternation by his host and by the ship's Duty Officer. "How the hell did you get aboard? We're loading gold bullion, and under close guard. Just be a pal and get out of here quietly the way you came, will you? There's a good chap." Irvin obliged, bidding good-night to the sentries on his way home, and reserving for later his opinions on the security services. On another occasion he wandered after dark and found himself in an area surrounded by barbed wire, confronted by a soldier with a levelled rifle, no

English, and a hostile disposition. Faced with Siberia or worse he fumbled nervously for a packet of Player's, proferred it to his challenger like a child handing buns to an elephant, and was rewarded with a beaming smile, directions – in English – to the nearest town, and the information that he had strayed within the compounds of a prisoner-of-war camp. Cigarettes may be bad for the lungs, but they pay their way in wartime.

Another, and quite different boost to morale and good relationships comes to Maurice Irvin's mind when he recalls one evening in the "Interclub" in September 1942, when the cold dark nights of winter were closing in, when the company consisted largely of survivors from *PQ 17*, and when not even the vodka or the orchestra could raise a genuine smile. In this case the saviour was not tobacco, but an American Marine who stalked into the Club, took one look around the assembled self-sympathisers, and bellowed "Right, you miserable lot – it's time I put you through your paces." He had a right to speak – no-one, at that time, visited Russia on American Express – and before they could protest he had riffled through the scratched records for some Souza marches and had the whole company drilling with a swing up and down the dance floor, obeying his every "*Hup*-two-three-four" till they were ready to drop in their tracks. In the weeks and months that followed, whenever spirits sagged, the men in the "Interclub", worn out and under bombardment, would march and counter-march till all thought of aircraft or submarines was forgotten, at least for the moment.

It was about this time, in mid-September, that *PQ 18* came into Archangel, the docks at Murmansk by now having been hammered by bombing almost out of existence. The convoy had lost thirteen out of its forty ships, but for Maurice Irvin there was the surprise of seeing amongst the survivors his very first sea-going vessel, the *Goolistan*, and the delight of discovering that its Chief Engineer, after eight years, was still the same officer with whom he had sailed in days of peace. The reminiscence, and the vodka, flowed free in the "Interclub" that night, but the cargoes were now pouring in thick and fast, and unloading of the tanks and other heavy vehicles was virtually non-stop.

By filling a note-book with phonetic translations Irvin had by now made himself proficient in basic Russian, at least in relation to the exigencies of his job, and he was well pleased with the work of the team he had assembled. Outstanding among them were some Russians of quite striking contrast. The work force was led by an aged patriarch named Ivanov, white-bearded and venerable, and the stars of the cast, in task performance as well as in physical charms, were two twenty-year-old twin girls, pretty and slightly built, but the equal of any man in the handling of the most sophisticated and important winches. The teams, in relays, worked long hours, and the vital supplies kept rolling along the jetties, and suddenly, to the surprise of the Merchant Navy contingent, the Russian authorities decided to show their appreciation by sending three invitations to each vessel for a banquet to be held in the International Club.

Maurice Irvin attended reluctantly, frankly expecting very little in the way of entertainment or culinary delight, but admits now that he was both wrong and churlish in his pre-assessment of Russian hospitality. A launch was sent around the ships to convey the guests to the scene of the festivities, where they were greeted by the Mayor of Archangel; as a specially assembled orchestra played them through the preliminaries they were ushered into the main hall, which at first they did not recognise. Long tables laid with spotless linen and heavy, opulent cutlery were bedecked with flowers, and the range of assorted glasses at each place-setting made an agreeable harbinger of what was to follow. For Irvin himself there was even the extra bonus of seeing Tanya flitting radiantly in the background, doing her bit as a helper before her later duties as a hostess.

One small incident threatened for a moment to mar the occasion. This banquet was being held as a gesture to the men who had been long engaged in the unloading of the war material and had been working in close co-operation with the Russian dockers and drivers. Just before the first course was to be served, there arrived uninvited a deputation, representatives of the survivors of various convoys, men who had been through a great deal and were far less than happy with the food and accommodation provided for them while they waited to join ship for the long voyage home. Each envoy carried a tin tray on which rested his meagre evening's meal, but happily their protest was made with commendable dignity and restraint. They simply marched up to the top table, where each laid down his ration, their spokesman saying quietly "Please add this to your feast – we are tired of it." They then retired without another word, their point made, and after a moment of silent embarrassment the banquet began. It was perhaps as well they did not linger, for as Maurice Irvin relates.

"It exceeded our wildest expectations. Really a feast to remember, the full five courses, with the glasses being replenished before they were half-empty, and again after every speech. We were told what jolly good chaps we all were, and how a telegram was being sent from the banquet to Uncle Joe – all the usual stuff, though there *was* one speaker out of the ordinary, a small, rather tubby man, with a good sense of humour that, through an interpreter, kept us amused. It turned out he was a very senior chap indeed, a Captain Papanin, one of the naval king-pins in Northern Russia; twice Hero of the Soviet Union, he had once voluntarily spent nine months on an ice-floe near the North Pole, charting the Polar currents. The drinks kept flowing, and the floor was cleared for dancing; I was damn glad, I don't mind telling you, of having Tanya's steadying influence as I tried to trip the light fantastic. And even then the celebrations weren't over; two days later they took us all to a show at a theatre, where a beautiful Russian brunette brought the house down by singing "Loch Lomond" and, for an encore, "Ramona." It was a marvellous interlude in a dreary and dangerous routine, and all in all the Russians had done us proud."

137

But the dangers and the realities were never far away. Only a few nights after the banquet Irvin and his friend George Gunn of the *Goolistan* were returning to their ships when they were caught in a heavy air raid; with so many ships unloading these were almost a daily and nightly hazard. This was really a severe one, and they dived under a railway truck for cover. Some time later, when the last of the bombs had dropped, they crawled out again, spitting and cursing and brushing the dirt from their persons and their clothing. Their concern for their shore-going uniform evaporated, however, when they took a closer look at the wagon under which they had sought shelter. It was loaded high with TNT. As to the realities, George Gunn's luck was not to last; two days later his convoy sailed out towards North Cape, and later Maurice Irvin learned that the *Goolistan* had been torpedoed and had sunk with all hands.

By early November the Arctic winter was drawing in tight, the hours of daylight were shortening, and Irvin knew that he and his shipmates must prepare to leave Bakaritsa and make for Murmansk before the White Sea froze over. It was time to issue and to test the Arctic clothing with which they had all been provided; "We had been well looked after – two sets of vests and Long Johns of the thickest wool I had ever seen, two pairs of sea-boot socks in the same material, knee-length boots made of leather, with wooden pegs, a fleecy-lined leather jerkin, a duffel-coat of wool and waterproof canvas, a Ku Klux Klan helmet with slits for eyes and mouth, and a sheepskin rug for the bunk, as well as sacks full of comforts from good souls at home – balaclavas, socks, mittens, sweaters, all sorts of useful things. I tried my underwear and it was just too scratchy and ticklish – I simply couldn't wear it. Before leaving I presented each of the twins with a vest and a pair of Long Johns, and honestly they were so overjoyed they'd have married me on the spot – both of them."

Life was harsh in Murmansk, but for Maurice Irvin there came an unexpected and wholly delightful Christmas present – in the arrival of his trained team from Archangel, led by Ivanov and the twins. With the old foreman he shared his Christmas dinner, which was accepted only after the cabin door had been locked; such was the fear of being reported for fraternising that a pilot would not even accept a cup of coffee in the saloon unless his colleagues did likewise. As for the two girls, they would slap a slice of black bread and dripping on to the winch cylinder, wait until it became a glutinous mass of hot grease, and then consume it with every evidence of enjoyment. Momentarily less pleasant for one of the twins was the occasion when the call of nature became pressing, leaving her no chance to go ashore. Irvin obligingly showed her the toilet compartment, but his Russian was not fluent enough to enable him to pass on clearly the warning that, as a necessary precaution against frozen pipes, the lavatory pan operated on scalding water. A startled squeal announced that the girl had discovered this for herself, but as she emerged smiling it was assumed she had suffered no irreparable damage.

A few days later another Russian woman distinguished herself under sterner circumstances. One air raid became so severe that the handlers, not Ivanov and his team, made a sudden bolt for the shore, which as Irvin says would have been reasonable enough but for the fact that in their haste they had left a thirty-eight ton tank hanging in mid-air from the forward boom, as great a hazard to the ship as any bomb, and not all his shouting would persuade them back on board.

"Then their foreman came up to me – one of the toughest looking women I have ever seen, with weather-beaten features and hands like spades – and said that if I would drive the winch, she would go down the hold, land the tank, and unshackle it. With bombs and shrapnel from the Ack-Ack guns falling all round her she did just that, cool as you please; when she came back on deck I hugged her, and she seemed all embarrassed. But I reported her bravery to the authorities, and I was delighted to learn later that she had been awarded a medal, for by God she had earned it."

Irvin next had occasion to reflect upon the best and the worst aspects of life in another Service, the Royal Navy. Early in 1943 the convoy *JW 51B* was attacked some two hundred miles from the entrance to the Kola Inlet not only by U-boats but also by the surface vessels, *Hipper* and *Lützow*, an action in which the British destroyer *Onslow* was severely damaged. Her captain, who refused to leave the bridge although badly wounded, was subsequently awarded the Victoria Cross. It was at this singularly inappropriate moment that the D.E.M.S. ratings, the naval gunners aboard the *Empire Elgar*, decided to protest vehemently about the arrogance of their Chief Petty Officer and about the treatment they received from him. Irvin, putting the problem down to boredom and stress, tried to pacify the men without undermining the PO's authority, but in the face of their insistence he eventually sent for the man – and quickly found that the complaints were fully justified.

"He even tried to put *me* in my place, sneering that he was Royal Navy whereas I was *only* M.N. Well, I reckoned that was a case for the Senior British Naval Officer, and as luck would have it, Captain Dickson came aboard at coffee-time. I discussed the matter with him in the saloon, and then he sent for the Petty Officer. He gave him a fair hearing, and then – my God, I have never heard anything like it in all my years at sea. It was like a barrage opening up, and it ended with the PO being ordered to smarten up his sloppy appearance and to stop making a bloody nuisance of himself. The SBNO then quietly left, saying no more than 'I don't think you'll have any further trouble there.' Magnificent."

Another senior officer to prove his worth as an ally was none other than Captain Papanin, who soon proved himself a Hero not only of the Soviet Union, but also of the British Merchant Navy. This incident started well, faltered badly, and ended splendidly. Captain Papanin, on an official visit to Murmansk, made a speech thanking the British seamen for their gallant contribution to the war effort, and everyone thought that was very agreeable of him until, at the last moment, he spoiled the whole effect by suddenly declaiming 'But it is not enough; we want more tanks, more planes – and *quicker discharge.*' It was the two final words that did the damage, and there were angry words amongst the crewmen before the Captain was ushered away to the privacy of the saloon, where Maurice Irvin, having made Papanin's acquaintance during the banquet at Archangel, took it upon himself to point out how tactless and ill-chosen the words had been in relation to men who were working all hours against frozen pipelines, inadequate unloading facilities, and without any of the shore amenities they had enjoyed at their earlier berths. Why, he pointed out, they could not even get a tot of vodka when off duty, and hadn't had a drink for many weeks. The following afternoon there was delivered, in Maurice Irvin's name "six of the biggest bottles I have ever seen containing spirits. They stood two feet six inches high, and their diameter was nine inches – you'd never *believe* there could be so much vodka in one place. We took it into bond, issued very generous tots to all hands on the first night, and thereafter doled it out like a Royal Navy rum ration. The consignment had been marked 'With the compliments of Captain Papanin' – a good democrat no doubt, but clearly a prince among men."

There was cheering again aboard the *Empire Elgar* at the end of January 1943, when the news arrived that the first ships of a new convoy had reached the Kola Inlet, and that aboard them was the relief for the *Elgar*'s crew. Irvin describes how everything was smiles and good humour, everyone was packing for home, when the first escort approached and made an official signal with its Aldis lamp. 'Reliefs are on their way' Cheers from the assembled crew. 'But regret the following must stay – two AB's, two firemen, one donkeyman, Second Engineer and First Mate.'

"I went numb, and could barely make acknowledgement; I had been acting First Mate for quite some time, but no promotion was ever worth *that* price. Still, my orders were definite, and so were the Second Engineer's; we could do nothing for ourselves, but we reckoned we might be able to help at least some of the lads. We had a meeting of all officers and decided we would represent to the Ministry of War Transport and to the new Master that under existing conditions, while we were not operational on a navigating basis, the retentions could safely be reduced to one AB, one Donkeyman, and the two officers. We read our message to the crew and told them to sort things out for themselves in ten minutes – choosing who should stay, if our request was granted, was something I was *not* prepared to undertake. When it came to the AB, seven pieces of paper were put in a hat, one of them marked with a cross; of course it had to happen – the lad who marked the papers, folded them, and offered his hat was the lad who drew the cross, the last slip to come out. He followed me to my cabin and just sat on the settee and sobbed, and I had to tell him I could make no promises but I would do my best. As it happened,

there was so much confusion when the new crew arrived I think I could have
got away with anything. When I sent for the boy and told him he was on his
way he started laughing like a lunatic, and I said to him 'Aye, you're
laughing now, you crying bugger' – but there was no malice in it. When at
last I watched these fellows sail for home I was damn near crying myself, and
I was a Chief Officer, not a deckie."

And so the Chief Officer and the Second Engineer were left to shake down
with a new crew, but even that had its compensations, for the necessity of
familiarising the new men with their duties kept both officers busy and left
little time for brooding. After one firmly intentioned booze-up on the night of
their comrades' departure on Convoy *RA 52*, they settled in to their
accustomed routine and forced themselves to consider their own relief simply
as something that would come in due course, a resolution that was
strengthened, and their disappointment softened, when they learned that the
officers who should have replaced them had given their lives en route for
Russia. In fact the waiting lasted no more than a few months, and at the end
of February Irvin took his farewells of Ivanov and the twins, and of many
other friends he found, almost to his surprise, that he had made during his
sojourn in the Arctic.

Two ships went down on the convoy in which he sailed, and he confesses
freely to a dread that after all his experiences he would never complete the
journey home, but at last he found himself back in West Hartlepool,
gradually unwinding from the strain in the understanding of parents and
sisters who saw him safely through the traumatic period of recuperation
leave, when the sound of a telephone would send him leaping from his chair.
He drank too much beer, and he found that when trying to write letters he
could concentrate for no more than a few minutes at a time, but one night
towards the end of March he discovered that the long nightmare was slowly
dissolving into memories.

"I met Pop one evening coming out of choir practice, and I asked him to
give me a tune on the organ. He knew well what I wanted, but first he
improvised slowly on soothing melodies and I sat there alone in the nave and
I thought of Ivanov, and about the twins, and about Tanya, but most of all
about those shipmates and comrades who hadn't returned, and as my mind
was musing about the *Empire Elgar*, I heard the organ, as if in the distance,
swell into crescendo, until the building vibrated and roused me from my
reverie to bring me back to this Land of Hope and Glory."

Chapter 24

THE FLOATING LATRINE

In May 1943 Captain H.W. Charlton, DSC, who had skippered the Commodore ship *River Afton* on the ill-fated Convoy *PQ 17*, found himself in another unsavoury situation, commanding the *Empire Envoy*, which had been designated as a prison ship. The Allied victory in the Western Desert was complete, and both Rommel's Afrika Korps and their Italian supporters were now simply thousands of prisoners of war, presenting a considerable problem in terms of both hygiene and accommodation.

The *Empire Envoy* had five holds, and Captain Charlton's estimate was that an adequate total of prisoners would be five hundred. The Army thought five thousand, and a compromise was reached – two thousand, some German, some Italian. Therein lay the immediate difficulty: the Italians crept aboard spiritless and dejected, the Germans arrogant as ever and singing the Horst Wessel – singing, that is, until they were shepherded down below and had the hatches battened down on top of them. Then, in the darkness, all hell broke loose, with the erstwhile allies screaming and fighting each other in a desperate scramble for the ladders leading, they hoped, towards fresh air, for all two thousand had suffered an urgent need to empty their bowels, and lavatory pans, though requisitioned, had not arrived.

"The arrogance evaporated, if that's the right word, during that long, hot, Algerian night, and Germans as well as Italians were soon screaming and moaning to be let out. The stench down there was disgusting, and even up in the cabins it was impossible to sleep. To make matters worse, especially for the Italians, we were attacked during the night by their own bombers, roaring on to us in low-level sorties out of Sicily, and when one bomb landed right alongside us, making the whole ship shudder, they were screaming in their terror down below."

Next morning Charlton made his protest to the authorities, and it was heeded; the German prisoners were sent back to their shore-based pen and replaced by a further contingent of Italian soldiers. Fresh water tanks were filled to their capacity of sixty tons, and another hundred tons were stored in the forepeak for ablutions, though there was no time to remedy the damage already done, and the new prisoners were sent down into holds stinking with their compatriates' excreta. They went down there under compulsion, urged by four armed guards with fixed bayonets.

The ship's destination was the United States, and it was not until an hour after she had left the Algerian port of Bône that it was discovered that the Army had failed to put on board, as ordered, the toilet drums so desperately needed. Captain Charlton knew, and now concedes, that he should have turned back, for conditions were, in his own words, inhuman, but this was wartime, and he sailed on westwards. After a night of horror the morning sun beat down on the steel decks, and the sounds from below became subdued. He ordered the hatches to be opened and the prisoners, under armed guard, to be allowed on deck. At first it was a limited, emergency procedure, with twenty-four very sick men being stretched out in a temporary sick bay beneath the poop awning, but almost immediately it became obvious that a much more dangerous situation was in the offing.

There was no doctor on board, and only four pints of 'settling' mixture. The smell of the ship had become unbearable, flies were swarming on heaps of human excrement, and the holds were no longer habitable. Food could not possibly be regarded as safe, and there was in the background the awful threat of typhoid or cholera at sea. The holds were thrown open, and the prisoners given the freedom of the upper decks and they came surging up in their hundreds. As they reached the fresh air, to a man they dropped their trousers and hung themselves tail-first over the rails; as Captain Charlton remarks in an uncharacteristic burst of humour, "they had met their waterloo."

Not even in wartime could these conditions be allowed to continue. The ship was diverted to Algiers, where the sick were taken ashore, and a signal sent ahead to Gibraltar to the effect that Captain Charlton, owing to the inhumane conditions, was unwilling to continue his assigned voyage. By return came a message instructing him to disembark his prisoners at Mers-El-Kebir, near the strategic port of Oran, where they would be held in a temporary camp pending their transport in suitable shipping to the United States.

On arrival at Mers-El-Kebir fifty luckless Italians were kept on board to clear up the Augean filth while the crew of the Empire Envoy played high-pressure hoses down the holds, and the ship then steamed to Gibraltar for scientific fumigation. Her next orders were to make for Rio de Janeiro to pick up a cargo of iron ore for Middlesborough. In the heartfelt words of Captain Charlton "The Trade Winds blew down the ventilators; the ship became sweet once more."

Chapter 25

CONWAY CADET

Between the Wars the adventure novels of Percy F. Westerman helped to send a great many impressionable boys to sea. Occasionally his romantic talent – as a magnificent story-teller – could have the opposite effect. Elsewhere in this book John Harding-Dennis describes his feelings of disillusionment when his introduction to the Merchant Navy, and to his first cabin, failed spectacularly to measure up to what Westerman's stories had led him to expect. Westerman's tales of derring-do had a less predictable effect on Peter Woolcott. He, from as far back as he can remember, had a burning ambition to emulate the feats of his boyhood heroes, not at sea, but in the air. All he wanted was to fly as a regular officer in the Royal Air Force, and his parents were willing and able to support him in his aim.

The outbreak of war put an end to all that. In 1940 young Woolcott, learned that the Royal Air Force College, Cranwell, was no longer accepting candidates for the Permanent Commission on which he had set his sights. He learned also, however, that it was possible to achieve Cadet Entry into the Royal Air Force through the training ship HMS *Conway*, and after passing a hastily-arranged entrance examination he duly presented himself as a Conway Cadet in January 1941, only to find out, too late, that the information fed to him had been faulty in one important detail. By this time *no* Permanent Commissions were being awarded in the Royal Air Force, and all that was being offered was wartime service.

For reasons that he still cannot explain he ignored the possibility of flying with the Fleet Air Arm, and resigned himself to making the best of an unsought-for career in the Merchant Navy. He did well on *Conway*, passing out eventually with an Extra Certificate, a Gold Medal, and several other prizes, and even before graduating from the training ship he had been brought face to face with the realities of war.

"We were at Birkenhead being re-fitted when the Blitz on Liverpool was at its worst, and we were soon hurried back to our usual moorings at Rock Ferry. During one night of exceptionally heavy air attack 13 March 1941, the watch spotted some object under a parachute falling into the water near the ship; reckoning this might well be a magnetic mine, and that when the tide turned we would swing right in towards it, the captain gave the order that all but a skeleton party of Seniors and staff were to abandon ship. Well, the *Conway* suffered no damage, but just after we had been put ashore, to sweat out the night in what I think was a disused dance-hall, another mine did do its work, and the *Tacoma City*, a five-thousand ton steamer, was blown to smithereens just two and a half cables from where the *Conway* was berthed. The fellows we had left on board put out the boats, and are said to have done a very fine job in picking up the survivors under fire."

Peter Woolcott learned, too, about *personal* loss while still a youngster trying hard to overcome his susceptibility to sea-sickness, a malady he was not to conquer until he was in his thirties, sailing "in a really vicious little ore-carrier." The personal tragedy, however, came much earlier than that, while he was still a cadet on *Conway*.

"My special friend was a genial red-head from Cumberland called Joe Payne, and he had already been accepted for entry into the New Zealand Shipping Company when his training was over. I thought this seemed a sound enough idea – nice ships, pleasant routes, not too posh, and I'd be joining with a good mate. I applied, and was told that I would be accepted when I left *Conway*. Great. Then, just a few weeks later, Joe and I were relaxing in the Main Top when the Duty Cutter was called away. I scuttled down the ratlines and into the boat: as we pulled away I heard a terrible cry as someone fell from the rigging. It was Joe, trying to slide down the Main Forestay to the deck; they tell me he had a sort of black-out halfway down, let go with his hands, and went head-first on to one of the hatches. Well, as an air raid precaution the hatches had been layered with concrete paving stones; he never came back to consciousness, and he died two days later. It was brutal bad luck, but I decided to carry on with our plan single-handed. Then came the next shock; the New Zealanders had lost so many ships that they would not be able to offer me a vacancy for another year. So I applied for acceptance as an Apprentice with the British Tanker Company, passed the interview, and spent a lot of time and money kitting myself out with the prescribed list of tropical whites, pith helmets, and what have you."

His first appointment was to the ten thousand ton *British Governor*, built in 1924 and therefore two years older than he was himself, and it very soon became apparent that his expenditure upon tropical whites and pith helmets had been money wasted, for she was sent to Cammell Laird's Shipyard to be fitted out with equipment and armament for duties in the Arctic. Insulation was fitted around the exterior bulkheads, steam heaters were installed, Gunners' accommodation was set up in the centre castle, Bofors guns were mounted on the foredeck and extra Oerlikons on the bridge. A barrage balloon was tethered on the afterdeck, six-months' supply of dehydrated fruit and vegetables crammed into the stores, and strange fittings attached to the

146

tanklids – a precaution, they were told, against the likelihood of their being shelled or torpedoed. The ship was to be employed as a Fleet Oiler, and the new devices were parts of a salvage system that would blow water out of the tanks should they be holed . . .

If all this preparation was faintly alarming, there were compensations for Peter Woolcott and the three other young apprentices assigned to the *British Governor*. First they found that by a recent BTC ruling they had been promoted from the time-honoured 'Glory Hole' next to the steering flat to the luxury of the midships staterooms that in quieter times had served to accommodate company executives on their voyages to the Persian Gulf. While the ship's officers were fetching their shaving water in buckets, the lowly apprentices could turn on the taps and treat themselves to hot baths. They also ate in the Officers' Saloon and were allowed, after seeking permission, to make use of the Smoking Room. Against these unwonted privileges, and just possibly because of them, they were subjected to merciless discipline by the First Mate, and even now Woolcott recalls with a tinge of bitterness the time when they were refused shore leave until they had pumped out the foredeck freshwater tank by hand. "It took what seemed days of arm-wearying work, while all that was needed, really, was to open the tap and let it run away. Still, in these days, apprentices were fair game."

Through some of the worst weather the Irish Sea has to offer, the *British Governor* sailed for Loch Ewe to join a convoy bound for Murmansk, and for days Peter Woolcott suffered the miseries of constant sea-sickness. "God, how I hated that Mate when I was ordered up to the Monkey Island to take an Azimuth; a simple exercise in the classroom became an almost impossible task. But I recovered in the serenity of the loch, with the stirring sight of all these ships at anchor and the Scottish mountains in the background. Most reassuring of all was the presence of the Anti-Aircraft Cruiser HMS *Scylla*, vast and imposing and bristling with guns, and it was good to know we would be sailing under her protection."

That protection was to be called for. Off Iceland the convoy was spotted by a Focke-Wulf Condor circling at high altitude, and from then on a reconnaissance aircraft was their constant companion. Their route took them far north, right up to Bear Island, but when they had passed there and come within reach of the German air bases, the attacks began, lasting from dawn to dusk on five successive days. After dark the onslaught would be taken over by U-boats. "At night we would hear and feel the thump of depth-charges, and it wasn't easy to lie fully dressed in your bunk and try desperately get some much-needed sleep, knowing that any minute might bring a torpedo. As for the air raids, the noise was simply indescribable. Flights of Stukas would come screaming down mingling with the crump of exploding bombs and the rattle and thunder of everything from Oerlikons and Bofors to the *Scylla*'s big guns. The sheer volume of fire put up was unbelievable; some measure of its power and accuracy may be gauged from the fact that throughout five days and nights of non-stop attack, not one single ship in that convoy was lost; we must have had charmed lives."

The voyage came to its end with the welcome sight of Russian destroyers and aircraft coming out to escort the merchantmen into the Kola Inlet, and Woolcott and his shipmates breathed a sigh of relief as they dropped anchor off the naval base at Vaenga. Their thankfulness was premature, for their real ordeal was just about to begin.

"The Kola Inlet is steep-to on one side and flat on the other, and the Russians decreed logically enough that ships awaiting discharge would have the protection of the cliffs while the empty vessels would anchor near the exposed bank. Fair enough, but by some weird twist of thinking the *British Governor*, with its tanks full of replacement oil, was classed as empty and moored accordingly. At first it wasn't the Germans that bothered us, but the Mate. We apprentices spent most of our time swinging ice-axes, trying in vain to keep pace with the sheets that covered the decks and rigging; that was bad enough, but at least we knew it was necessary, against the danger of the ship's becoming top-heavy. But that man actually put us to scrubbing the deck around the master's cabin *with cold water*, in the middle of an Arctic winter."

Woolcott, with his interest in aviation still undiminished, found enjoyment in watching the Hurricanes of the Red Air Force and in repeatedly discouraging the Radio Officer, who had a gunnery watch, from directing his fire on them under the impression that they were Messerschmitts. "Then one Sunday morning, just after breakfast, I heard a rattle of fire coming along the line of ships, and I stuck my head out of a porthole just in time to see a real ME 109 releasing two bombs as it flashed over us from the bow. I woke up to find myself lying in the cross alleyway with all hell let loose around me. There were jets of steam everywhere and the whistle was blowing like crazy; we were listing heavily to port and were way down by the head; the hold was flooded and all the Red Cross clothing ruined, though it helped with the buoyancy, and all the plating was caved in for'ard of the collision bulkhead. It seemed at first that the concave shape had saved the main body of the vessel; what we didn't realise at the time was that the concussion of the bombs – a perfect straddle – had split the hull clean across, and that there was only about six inches of keel plate holding the whole ship together.

"Incredibly, she didn't sink, and that was when our special extra salvage gear proved its worth. In an astonishingly short time the compressed air pipes had us floating once again on an even keel, and after lunch we were sitting in the Smoking Room listening to the radio when we had the great satisfaction of hearing Lord Haw Haw announce that the *British Governor* had been sunk in the Kola Inlet."

Long weeks and months in Arctic waters now lay ahead of them, for the damage to the ship was in fact great, and Peter Woolcott settled down to the time-honoured task of staving off boredom in wartime. He learned to speak fairly fluent Russian, and no doubt it was through this very un-British accomplishment that he came into far greater and far friendlier contact with these allies than did most seamen who spent months in the country. Despite certain restrictions, he met and mingled with the local citizens in Vaenga, Murmansk, and later in Archangel, and, perhaps most surprisingly of all, his particular friends were the NKVD guards permanently stationed at the gangways. "After all" he explains, "they were only sixteen-year-old youngsters like myself. I've often wondered what has become of them since then."

Woolcott and some of his shipmates added a touch of sartorial splendour by sacrificing their lambswool blankets, which a local tailor fashioned into fur hats, *chapkas*, and which looked very smart, if somewhat unorthodox, with a Merchant Navy badge stitched to them. Like everyone else they engaged regularly in barter, and when the summer months came they were able to enjoy a pleasant social life ashore in Archangel, where they went regularly to clubs and hotels, theatres and cinemas. Peter Woolcott certainly does not regret the time he spent in Russia, for he took a real interest in the affairs and customs of a strange country, but it was not until November that the *British Governor* at last received her sailing orders, and after ten months abroad he and the rest of the crew were happy to be on their way home. Their return voyage might well have ended in tragedy, for severe storms in the White Sea stove in the temporary plating on the bows, and the ship had to leave the convoy and stagger back to England unescorted and at greatly reduced speed. She managed the trip, but so visible was the damage she had suffered that to their delight the entire crew were presented, without having earned it, with an entire new outfit of clothing, the gift of the Shipwrecked Mariners' Society; perhaps they were not strictly entitled to it, but it would be a churlish man indeed who grudged them this little stroke of luck.

The next assignment for the ex-Conway Cadet was to the brand new MACship, the *Empire MacCabe* commanded by a master, Captain Mac-Michael, for whom Peter Woolcott has nothing but the highest praise and who was subsequently to become Commodore of the BTC Fleet. "He was a wonderful person who befriended and encouraged every man aboard, and thanks to him it was a really happy ship. I was thrilled, of course, to be on a vessel carrying three aeroplanes – Swordfish – on her deck, and as my main duties were as assistant to the Chief Yeoman of Signals I was very much a part of the flying programme and often the very first person to learn what was going on. Our aircrews were New Zealanders, a grand crowd, and I learned that it was a background of barnstorming that had given them their remarkable skills in landing on a twelve-thousand ton ex-tanker with a flight deck not much bigger than a couple of tennis courts. They had their mishaps, of course, and a few undercarriage oleos paid the price of heavy landings; once there was a pile-up that could have been very nasty indeed. The last aircraft came in with a hell of a bump, bounced clean over the trip-wires, and sliced off his starboard wingtip on the mast just two feet above my head. He crashed into the other two aircraft, and the whole lot of them burst into flames. On that of all days the Armourer, against all regulations, had left the magazine open for an airing, and next minute gallons of blazing petrol were pouring down the ammunition hoist. Incredibly, not one person was even injured."

There was to be no such miracle of good fortune attending a later incident, when the ship was bound for Halifax, Nova Scotia. The Swordfish were normally armed with rockets, the most effective weapons against the U-boat, and these were not off-loaded when the aircraft were parked, for the action of folding back the wings automatically broke certain electrical circuits and so rendered the firing mechanism safe. "One day an Observer was making an extra check of his radio gear, and he was sitting in his cockpit, while a routine servicing was being carried out on the firing equipment of the adjoining aircraft. Well, something went terribly, tragically wrong, a rocket suddenly fired, and that poor fellow was literally cut clean in half. It was awful, and it may sound callous to say that the outcome could very easily have been much worse than it was, but that is the simple truth. The rocket, you see, just passed clean through the Observer as if he didn't exist, and it only just missed a loaded tanker on our starboard beam. A few feet to one side and it would probably have accounted for every man aboard her."

There were other incidents less gruesome, and to the air-minded Peter Woolcott there were the delights of occasional joy-rides in the Swordfish when the ship was berthed in Canada. These same aircraft might also have been involved in one of the most sensational blunders of all time. In mid-Atlantic the *Empire MacCabe* was thrilled to encounter no less a vessel than the *Queen Elizabeth*; as a matter of routine the MACship issued an orthodox challenge, and interest turned to consternation when the liner failed to make the correct signal in acknowledgement. Captain MacMichael hurriedly consulted higher authority, and was given the almost unbelievable instruction to mount an air strike against the pride of the Cunard Fleet. It was a direct order, and he had no choice but to have the Swordfish rockets replaced by aerial torpedoes, but one can only wonder at what must have been going through his mind as he desperately repeated his challenge before sending the aircraft into action, and one is bound to speculate, too, as to whether any of these young New Zealand pilots would actually have aimed their torpedos at the most famous passenger liner afloat. But this was one military disaster that happily did not occur; someone aboard the *Queen Elizabeth* finally awoke to the real situation, and the correct signal of the day came flashing over at what we may imagine was her Yeoman's very fastest rate.

After a year aboard the *Empire MacCabe*, Peter Woolcott felt a distinct sense of anticlimax when ordered to join the orthodox twelve thousand ton tanker *Empire Integrity*, but in fact the most frightening stage of his personal war at sea still lay ahead of him. He had been between ships when the D-Day landings took place, and so he had missed the excitement and danger of those, and had been engaged in carrying aviation spirit to and fro across the Atlantic, but now the *Empire Integrity* was ordered to carry a cargo of motor fuel into Antwerp, and although that city was in Allied hands, the islands in the Scheldt Estuary most certainly were not. "Maybe the Old Man knew what to expect, but I did not, even though I was now sailing as 3rd Mate; I suppose I might have guessed, when the Belgian pilot came aboard in Thameshaven, but I didn't, until we arrived off the Scheldt and stopped engines. We drifted in on the tide because of the danger of pressure mines, and any piece of floating debris was promptly peppered with small arms fire just in case.

"We were no sooner into the river than fog settled in thick and constant, and we lay at anchor for three or four days. During this time we kept hearing strange whooshing and thumping noises, but in our happy ignorance we paid no real attention to them, and couldn't understand why the Belgian pilot was looking so damned apprehensive. Then the fog lifted, and we moved into a lovely tanker berth almost in the city centre; we thought this was wonderful, perfect for a few hours ashore whenever possible. Our euphoria lasted perhaps an hour before we learned at last the secret of those background noises; the RASC boys who were unloading us told us cheerfully that they came from the German V-1 and V-2 rocket launching sites at Walcheren, and that those missiles not aimed against England were nicely zeroed in on the very spot where we were sitting on top of twelve thousand tons of petrol; that wiped the happy grins off our faces, I can tell you."

The *Empire Integrity* made three such runs to Antwerp, always with a sense of understandable anxiety amongst the crew, and Woolcott and his friends became quite knowledgeable about the behaviour patterns of the doodlebugs and their bigger brothers, the V-2s. "These V-2s were real brutes, and we would stand on the bridge and actually watch them being launched. If the vapour trail bent away from the vertical, it was on the way to London, and we could breathe again. If it went straight up it was headed for us, and we had perhaps sixteen or seventeen seconds to take cover if there was any. One day, when most of the crew were ashore in a *bistro* just outside the dock gates, the Mate, the pumpman, and myself were standing over one of the tanks, watching it drain, and we heard the noise of a V-1 being launched, but from our position we couldn't see it. Suddenly it appeared right over the funnel – and cut out. We raced aft like greyhounds and saw it pass on to explode a little way ahead of us, and then we just looked at each other in sheer disbelief – our sprint for safety had taken us to a spot directly over the magazine. We were still there when the boys ashore came up running; they'd heard the explosion and were very surprised to find they still had a ship to come to. And on another occasion, some enthusiastic RAF lad tried to tip the wing of a rocket two hundred feet above us, but luckily he didn't succeed, or that would have been the end of the *Empire Integrity*."

Instead, it was the end of her experience under fire. Once again she was ferrying fuel across the Atlantic, but now her destination was Italy, where the fighting had ended, and where Peter Woolcott and his shipmates were royally entertained ashore by both the British and the United States armies in a series of goodwill gestures towards the seamen who for so long and so dangerously had kept the soldiers supplied.

Chapter 26

THE HAS-BEEN

Sidney Cercell, after more than forty years at sea, now lives with his wife in a bungalow in the grounds of Springbok-Radcliffe Farm, a working establishment in Surrey run by the Merchant Seamen's War Memorial Society mainly for the rest, retirement, and rehabilitation of seamen who for some reason have come either temporarily or permanently ashore, and he was less than delighted during a discussion one day when a much younger resident remarked brutally of him and his contemporaries "Don't forget you are a lot of old has-beens." It was not difficult to persuade him to tell something of the circumstances, other than advancing years, that had qualified him for this derisive cataloguing.

"In the late 'twenties, after the General Strike, the Shipping Companies were building new fleets and looking for men capable of working the new machinery; well, I'd served my apprenticeship on this sort of stuff, and so I started on a career at sea. These were the days of the luxury liners, and prosperity showed everywhere in the shipping world – except, of course, in the seamen's wages. Still, it was work.

"Then came 1939, and everything changed, with fitters crawling everywhere, installing guns in previously prepared positions, and Marines coming aboard from Portsmouth to form us into teams and teach us how to use them. I was on the *Winchester Castle*, and up to the time of Dunkirk we were employed in transporting food and other materials. But after that we were taken over by Combined Operations and sent up to the lochs of Scotland, where Commandos and other troops were being trained as assault groups; our job was to put them ashore at the right places and, sometimes, to wait and re-embark them.

"After the training came the real thing, but our first jobs were simply trooping, though that could be exciting enough. Things were going badly for Britain in and around the Mediterranean, and the men destined to fight in the desert had to be taken around the coast of South Africa and up the Indian Ocean to Port Suez – practically the whole of the 8th Army were shipped like that, usually in convoys of fourteen to twenty ships carrying anything from three-thousand to five-thousand men apiece. Once they'd reached South Africa they would be split into groups of three or four vessels for easy servicing at the main ports from Cape Town to Durban."

Eventually, however, the British fight-back became reality, and in May 1942 the *Winchester Castle* reverted to her role of carrying assault troops. This time her mission was not just practice, but the landing of the initial invasion force in Madagascar. The ship lay there until the main occupying troops had arrived to relieve the assault party, whose survivors then came back on board, leaving their landing-craft behind them.

"We took these lads on to India, and they, poor fellas, ended up in Burma. As for us, we limped across two oceans to New York with a damaged propeller and only two lifeboats – the others had been dispensed with to make room for the assault craft – and after refitting and repair we made our way back to the West of Scotland to start the business all over again.

The business, this time, was coincidental with and contingent upon the decisive swinging of the fortunes of war in favour of the Allies, both on land and on the sea. While the men of the *Winchester Castle* were once again helping to put assault troops through their training paces on the Scottish coastline, their previous passengers, the 8th Army, were driving Rommel and the Afrika Korps to defeat in the Western Desert. Montgomery had achieved his triumph at El Alamein, and German troops were streaming westwards as the 8th Army moved forward to the recapture of Cyrenaica and Upper Tripolitania. In terms of naval supremacy there were developments of no less significance and immediate importance.

During the first few days of November 1942 German Naval Intelligence, for once, completely misread the reports that were submitted and the activities that could be seen all around the Middle East theatre of war. At a time when Allied assault convoys were already in the Mediterranean, and when there was an unusual degree of activity around and in Gibraltar, Dönitz was employing the main strength of his U-boat force in the harassment of convoys in the Atlantic. When the naval activity at Gibraltar was reported, German Intelligence dismissed it as no more than preparation for yet another Malta convoy, and not even the sighting of the fleet in the Straits alerted them to what was actually afoot, the Allied invasion of North Africa. The news was actually broken to them at the same time as it was to the rest of the world, when a BBC announcement gave the fleet's destination as Algiers.

This announcement entailed no breach of security, for it was not made until 8 November, the day chosen for a massive simultaneous attack by the assault forces of Britain and the United States on three separate ports, Algiers, Casablanca, and Oran: these were no mere raiding parties, but armies comprising some seventy thousand highly trained combat troops supported by commensurate supplies of ammunition, food, and fuel. It was not until noon on the chosen day that the enemy mounted the first air attacks on the convoys, and by then it was too late, although, in the words of Sidney Cercell, who was there all through the action, "the sight of the whole naval fleet fighting off the air raids was something never to be forgotten, more frightening even than the rocket attacks that were used in later landings; there's something very special about a battleship loosing off with all its guns, something no-one will ever see again."

The landings were effected with complete success and, as happened so often during the war, Adolf Hitler personally intervened with a contribution to the Allied cause. This he achieved on 11 November, just three days after the initial landings, when he ordered against the advice of his Generals the establishment of a bridgehead in Tunisia. His orders were of course obeyed, with the result that two Italian Divisions and three German Divisions, one of them armoured, were assigned to a hopeless task that achieved no more than a few months' delay in the inevitable outcome. These troops were committed from the outset to fighting on the retreat, and in attempting to keep them in even basic supplies the sailors of both Germany and Italy were subjected to grievous losses at the hands of the Allied air and naval forces who now found themselves, at last, in the role of attackers rather than defenders. Fleet Air Arm Albacores based on Malta, and the cruiser-destroyer forces Q and K, out of Bône and Malta respectively, wrought havoc with the shipping that was trying desperately to keep the Axis forces alive with fuel and ammunition, and once again the Mediterranean was a maritime graveyard – only this time the victims were not the Allied convoys trying to battle their way through to Malta.

While all this was going on the *Winchester Castle* had resumed her now familiar role in the training of assault troops, but now, instead of the Scottish lochs, her base was Suez and her proving ground the Gulf of Akabar. "We hardly thought of ourselves as civilians any more; after all, we had about twenty-five guns mounted by this time, and with sixty naval and army gunners as well as our own teams, we were able to give a pretty good account of ourselves during the air attacks."

They took part in the Sicily landings, lying off shore and watching a fair proportion of the airborne troops being dropped into the sea instead of on land – and while doing so they experienced a moment of their own in which they felt their time was up. "We were caught full in the beam of a searchlight on the shore, and we shook hands with each other and said our goodbyes, but our old friends the Commandos were already in there and they damn soon took care of that situation for us."

And so to Naples, where the *Winchester Castle*, as part of a newly-formed Task Force, took aboard a party of US Rangers and carried them into action on the Anzio beach-head. "That was our first experience of an attack with rocket missiles, and the noise was so terrific as they whooshed off that we found ourselves, unwillingly, crouching down on the deck. There were others, though, who *really* had something to worry about. Wynford Vaughan Thomas was with us, covering the thing as a reporter for the BBC, just as if it was a Royal Wedding or a football match, and he went in with the first wave of assault. Well, things were pretty hot at Anzio, and every now and again the troops were pulled back as relief from the heavy firing in the front line. But not poor Wynford Vaughan Thomas - he was stuck there on his own from start to finish, with no relief. I don't know why, but we all thought it rather funny at the time, though God knows it must have been no joke for him."

Yet they came out of it safely, both the merchant vessel and the BBC reporter, and after Anzio the pressure, at least for the moment, was off. "It seemed to us that there was nothing left but the Big One: the convoys were once again coming through the Suez Canal instead of all the way around, and our thoughts began to turn towards home. We had been away for close on two years, and what with stories of the bombs falling on our home towns, and maybe on our families, the men were starting to show signs of strain. We were being used to take troops here and there in the Med., and every time we joined a convoy heading for Gib. we thought this was it - but no, as soon as we got as far as Algiers or Oran, into port we used to go, and tempers wore very thin and scratchy."

That problem was intensified on the *Winchester Castle*'s very next operational assignment. "We were part of another Task Force, and again we were taking on American troops, but this time it was different. The gear was there all right, all the equipment needed by assault forces, but the men themselves - well, we'd been through it, and it was obvious that they just weren't trained like the troops we'd known before. More than that, there were terrible errors: we saw, for instance, that the Operations Room, which always before had been Holy Ground, was often left wide open, and not only that - stuck there for all to see was a huge map with arrows pointing to the south coast of France. Security? - God Almighty.

"But just the same we sailed, moving very slow, though after a few hours we turned back again; then we sailed again. This went on time after time until after about three days we learned the truth. The Allied Forces had landed in Normandy, and our deliberate decoy operation, with all its slack security, had caused the Germans to deploy between eight and ten-thousand troops to fight us off on the Riviera. That still left us time, of course, to take part in the real thing, and we went in as a back-up team with Free French troops aboard this time, but by this stage we had a new skipper who frankly was a bit bomb-happy and would insist on ordering a smoke-screen at the slightest sign of danger. Well, he did this just as the Frenchmen were making their way to the beaches of their native land, and the poor fellows got lost entirely and were completely out of the hunt.

"That's about all the wartime experience this old has-been picked up, apart of course from the subs, the sinking ships, and the picking up of survivors - but no, there is just one other memory, and maybe it's the most

156

important of the lot. One day off Algiers a German airman baled out of his aeroplane, and he was blazing on fire all the way down to his death – and we all watched him, and we cheered like madmen – which I suppose, come to think of it, we were. Maybe these youngsters could think about that for a minute – we, and that airman, were about the same age as they are now."

Chapter 27

"SHARK"

When relating the facts |contained in this story, Chief Officer Stanley Simpson, a man well known to the Seafarers Education Service, expressed the wish that the name of the ship involved in it be omitted, for even after the passage of many years he had no wish to risk causing renewed distress to any relatives of of those who lost their lives. It seems sufficient, therefore, to state simply that it was a vessel of the Strick Line, in which he sailed for many years, and that the facts of the incident are beyond dispute.

"I was on the bridge when the torpedo struck, and it was the loudest sound I had ever heard. A great column of water threw the matchwood of the starboard boats high into the air, and the fall of debris seemed interminable. We lurched heavily to port, and with a strange clarity my mind recorded that this must be what the textbooks call 'the initial heel', for by the time I reached the rail we were on an even keel again, and we managed to get the two remaining boats away quickly and without panic."

Chief Officer Simpson took command of one lifeboat, the ship's master being aboard the other, and a tally of heads told them that the losses had been severe. Two officers, three engineers, two radio operators, six gunners, and the entire engine-room watch – nineteen men in all were missing. But the ship was still afloat – just – and the Chief Officer decided he must go back on board and look for any injured survivors.

"The Captain called to me from the other boat 'you'd better be quick, Mister – she's going fast', and then another voice piped up. 'Let me come too, sir.' It was the Senior Cadet in the skipper's boat. Two days earlier he had celebrated his seventeenth birthday. The Captain and I looked silently across at each other for a long moment, and then he nodded his head. 'Off you go, son', he said quietly.

"The stern was almost awash when we climbed back on board, and I directed the boy to the wrecked cabins on the starboard side while I made for the engine-room. The silence was sepulchral, accentuated rather than diminished by the strange sound, like water over a weir, as the sea poured into the dying ship. In the dark and tangled chaos down below I could find only one body, and that mutilated beyond hope or redemption, and it was a relief to come away from the stench of oil and explosives and into the fresh air. The boy looked sick and white – God knows what sights *he* had encountered, for he simply shook his head and said nothing. The stern was completely submerged now, and we could feel the deck falling away beneath us as we slipped over the side and started swimming. We had not gone far, just out of danger from suction, when a great rumbling crescendo of sound drew our eyes back to the awesome sight of the ship in her death-throes. About a hundred feet of her bow was steepling straight upwards, trembling with the noise and the stress as the great engines, the boilers, the anchors and the cables tore their way through the bowels and the heart of her. Then she just slid away from us in a boiling of white foam."

The lifeboats seemed very small and distant, and at one point, as the pair of them struck out strongly, Stanley Simpson unwittingly pulled a few yards ahead of his young companion, until the boy called out 'Don't leave me, sir.' The Chief answered 'why should I leave you now, son?', and dropped back to swim alongside him. Then, in anguish, he realised what perhaps the cadet had already seen. The two lifeboats were rowing, not towards them but away from them, the survivors obviously having decided that they had gone down with the ship. After what seemed an age one of their shipmates finally spotted them, and the boats put about, but by now the boy was in real difficulties, almost unconscious and vomiting feebly as Simpson towed him slowly towards safety. Then anguish turned to terror.

The Cadet, being heaved along helplessly on his back, cried out suddenly 'Oh Christ – a shark', and Stanley Simpson experienced the worst moments by far of his long and adventurous life at sea.

"I had known fear before, and was to know it many times again, but dear God, never anything even remotely like this. There was the sour, metallic taste of pure terror in my mouth as I pulled the lad along, and I gradually took in that we were being circled not by one shark, but by three. The first attack had a nightmare illusion of slowness – no sudden rush, but a deliberate head-on approach of quite indescribable horror. I struck out with my free hand, and felt the dreadful solidity of the shark's head as it swirled past, grazing the skin right off my arm from wrist to shoulder. I vaguely heard shouting, and I kicked out even more desperately. The boy was taken only ten feet from the boat, and I did not even see him go. Just a violent wrench as he was torn from my grasp, a sudden rusty staining of the sea, and a confusion of yelling voices and flailing oars as I was dragged inboard – that was all. Just a few moments of black nausea, and then I found myself with work to do, and in a hurry."

Without the slightest concession to the ordeal he had just been through, this magnificent officer at once transferred himself to the role of ship's surgeon, cleaning, swabbing and stitching the awful abdominal wounds of one of the gunners who had been all but disembowelled in his mid-ships turret. Sadly this second life-saving attempt was also in vain, for the man died as the last suture was tied, and reluctantly, though indeed they had no choice, his shipmates cast him over the side.

To equalise the numbers, six men were directed for transfer from Simpson's boat, which with twenty-eight aboard was heavily overloaded, to the master's, which with fifteen was not, but the transfer never took place. The sea was now choppy, and as the two boats crashed together and then fell away, the first man ready to go was toppled overboard and was dragged back terrified just as a black fin came swooping in towards him. No-one argued when the Chief Officer, gazing at the brute with loathing, called to the Captain 'We're losing time, sir; let's just get out of here.'

The two boats set course independently for Tobago, eight hundred and twenty miles to leeward, and the master's crew, the lighter cargo, was already far ahead when darkness fell. It was never seen again. The moon rose early, and Stanley Simpson, at the tiller, steered mechanically with the breeze broad on the starboard quarter. Ahead of him the men lay curled in foetal positions of total exhaustion, but he himself had never in his life felt more wide awake.

"My mind was a tumbling turmoil of the events of the day, and the anguish of the boy's death pressed heavily upon me, as it was to do for a long long time to come. I felt a small hand upon my arm, and I looked down into the face of the little monkey that was snuggling into my side, mewing softly and gazing at me with those sad sad eyes. She had belonged to one of the radio men, now dead, and she still wore the preposterous little life-jacket that Sparky had fashioned for her. Her gentleness and affection, the trust of this tiny creature, touched some chord inside me, and I suddenly felt my eyes hot with unaccustomed tears. I was glad of the darkness around me."

At daybreak, as the men woke up, Sparky's monkey began making her rounds, jumping into each lap and gazing earnestly into each face, chittering endlessly as if in concerned enquiry after her master, and soon the Chief Officer was listening to the welcome sound of laughter in the boat. He was right in his guess that their small fellow-sufferer would prove invaluable as an aid to morale during the weeks ahead, and not once, even at the worst times, did any of the survivors even think of querying the common decision that the little marmoset should draw her rations like the rest of them. In fact she at first appeared somewhat less than grateful, grumbling morosely over her unaccustomed diet, but later she developed a positive passion for Horlicks tablets, and would unwrap the wax papers in a deep concentration of anticipation and delight.

Simpson's most valuable possession was the waterproof bag that seldom left his side when he was at sea and that contained his sextant, his tables, and other elementary aids to navigation, and his stroke of good fortune was that his wrist-watch had survived the explosion and the long immersion in the sea.

He was thus able to give a daily account of progress and prospects, which helped the men to keep their spirits high and to co-operate willingly and conscientiously in the routine of tasks that he set for them. Two watches of four hours on, four off, were to be maintained, the boat was at all times to be kept baled and clean, the sail and all other gear to be nursed carefully against wearing and chafing. He warned the men that they must expect at least a fortnight of waiting before they could even hope to sight land, and he warned them, too, about possible disappointments, such as ships that might pass without seeing them. But he explained also about the trade winds and the normally favourable currents, and he succeeded in passing on to them his own unquenchable faith and belief that they would win through.

By the morning of the third day they had made one hundred and thirty miles from the scene of the sinking, the heavily-laden boat lumbering along at three knots before a freshening breeze, but at noon the sky darkened and the horizon thickened to a menacing inky monochrome as the sea-rim closed in on them.

"The lug-sail was lowered and furled, and the conical sea anchor dropped to haul her head round to wind, and not a moment too soon. The horizon was hissing as it rushed towards us, and great drops of almost glutinous water came pattering into the boat like lumps of fat; then the full fury of the squall was upon us, lashing rain and tossing seawater driving over the bow as the little craft pitched and strained against the drag of the sea-anchor. We baled as if demented, yet still the water rose to our knees, and we were hard put to it to stay afloat. I felt truly thankful that I had not yielded to my initial temptation to gain distance by running before the wind."

By nightfall the wind had moderated, but still the rain poured down on them, and now every spare foot of canvas was spread to receive it and every cup and beaker filled to the brim as each man drank to the point of repletion. A soaked and shivering ship's company greeted the dawn, but their spirits rose with the sun and with their gratitude for the newly-filled tanks, and for the first time since the explosion there came the sound of singing; a few shy voices began it, but before long every man in the lifeboat was joining in a serious of rousing choruses. A week later they had made nearly four hundred miles towards Tobago, but never had they progressed further than fifty miles in any one day, and for the first time Stanley Simpson began to feel slight misgivings over the dwindling supplies of food, and the possible effect of extreme hunger upon the men's morale, especially during the night watches, when the sense of loneliness and desolation bore down most severely. He turned once more to the life-saving satchel that contained his sextant.

"Amongst the other treasures there was an anthology of English verse from which I drew immeasurable solace; even poems that I had long known by heart revealed new significance and dimensions in this environment of private fears and hopes and loneliness. One morning I read some of them aloud to the men, and without a dissenting voice they asked for more. Now most of these fellows had always regarded poetry as the province of the long-haired, limp-wristed, and effeminate, and their memories were of dreary hours spent learning by heart a screed of words in which they had not the slightest interest, simply in order to stay out of trouble at school. But here things were different, and it was good to see the impact of "The Lotus Eaters" or the "Ode on a Grecian Urn" upon minds that had been made receptive to the sheer beauty of language, for the first time, in this crucible of adversity."

By the nineteenth morning the boat had made more than seven-hundred miles, and though five of the men had been reduced to almost constant sleeping, the company was still intact, saved by the frequent showers that had kept them always with at least *some* ration of water, and by the discipline that had ensured that both they and the boat were as clean as the primitive conditions would allow. It was a source of private satisfaction, and no doubt of very justifiable private pride, to the Chief Officer that after nearly three weeks there had been not one single case of sickness. Yet now, within a hundred miles of their destination, he was beset by a deep and constant worry that could not, that must not, under any circumstances, be shared.

"During these days, as we neared the Indies, I could manage sometimes to put my fears aside, but during the night watches the incubus of terror would not be exorcised. Not one ship had been sighted, and the men spoke often of an obsession that daily pressed harder upon their minds – a sad belief that this small boatload of lonely souls was the only human life upon a vast and hostile sea. Now Tobago is of course an island, and my calculations for longitude depended entirely upon the accuracy of my timepiece. My mind turned all too frequently to the possibility of a major mistake. A single minute of error on the watch meant an error of nearly fifteen miles in the distances plotted on the chart. Too far behind would be disappointing; too far ahead could spell irretrievable and final disaster. For days I had kept to the middle latitude of Tobago, and that calculation I was sure of, because it had no relevance to time-keeping. But I was haunted during the night watches by visions of running between the islands in the dark, and so on and on into the broad Caribbean, with no hope of beating the boat back against the prevailing wind and current."

During the final days of the voyage, for Stanley Simpson those fears became a torment from which he could find no respite. Though desperately weary, he could no longer sleep; during the days he scanned the horizon eagerly for sight of land, and throughout the nights he strained his ears for the sound he dreaded to hear, the deep diapason of surf breaking upon a distant shore. He dreaded, too, the moment that could not much longer be postponed, the time when he must make a definite prediction to the men under his care and his command. The five weakest were now almost comatose; the others were alternately optimistically excited and dangerously depressed. In the event, that moment was decided for him.

Afternoon observations of the sun on the twenty-first day made the island only forty-six miles ahead. As he silently folded his chart and returned it to the satchel he was conscious of the men's eyes fixed hungrily, pleadingly upon him, and at last one of them spoke up. "When will we see land, sir?", voicing the question in every mind. He took a deep breath, and replied as matter-of-factly as he could. "I think tomorrow."

All that night he crouched at the tiller, unable to rest although craving for sleep, and he told the watch to listen for the slightest sound of breakers, scarcely a necessary instruction under the circumstances. As the dawn came creeping up from astern and spread over and ahead of them, the survivors gazed steadily to westward, and at last they could make out a faint grey smudge of cloud on the horizon. But it was not a cloud, it was land – it was Tobago.

"All that day the island changed perceptibly in both size and colour as we crept up on it, but at nightfall we were still ten miles short. The sail was lowered and we lay-to throughout the hours of darkness, and the men talked the whole night through, with laughter and singing breaking out every now and again. To my astonishment, I felt no great sense of elation at reaching the journey's end, only a feeling of vast contentment and peace. I was like a rocket spent.

"At daylight the island was noticeably nearer, and it was clear that the current here set strongly to the shore. The blue hills turned to green, and the outlines of palm trees emerged slowly from the haze of distance. I pushed up the tiller and headed for the northern point of the island, and by noon the white line of the surf could be seen fringeing the shore for as far as the eye could reach, while the grim thundering of the breakers hammering on the beach had a menacing note when heard from seaward.

"But as the boat neared the northern point, and opened the land behind, our weary eyes were greeted by a marvellous vista of waving, green-topped palms, and a foreshore white as snow. We turned the point, into a bay that had the unreal beauty of a picture from a children's story-book. Quietly, slowly, I steered the lifeboat across the sparkling transparency of calm water, until at last her stem was resting on the sand."

Chapter 28

FROM 1916 TO 1982

In Great Britain's Year of Maritime Heritage, with the men of the Merchant Navy, at the time of writing, once again giving their service and their lives in support of the armed forces in the South Atlantic, one is brought back inescapably to the realisation that as a power Great Britain can neither succeed nor survive without the dedication to duty of the merchant seamen upon whom supplies and movement in war must ultimately depend.

Of the many men who willingly gave their time to the recounting of the episodes contained in this story there are those who saw service not only in the Second World War, but in the First, and often, during the later conflict, it was their steadiness under pressure, that set a life-saving example to their younger shipmates. Errington Angus is now eighty-one years of age, and his sea-going years stretch from 1916, when he was an Assistant Steward aboard the *Greatham*, to 1961, when he reluctantly came ashore to retirement. Twenty six years before the tragic debacle of *PQ 17*, the *Greatham* sailed for Archangel out of Blyth in Northumberland with a cargo of four thousand tons of coal, and as she crept out into the North Sea she was joined by other ships, including a much larger vessel, the cruiser HMS *Hampshire*. Young Errington Angus and his shipmates were to be unwitting witnesses to one of the turning moments of military and maritime history. For the *Hampshire* was not only carrying supplies to support Britain's Russian allies on the Eastern Front, but a military mission headed by the Secretary of State for War Lord Kitchener. On 5 June 1916 *Hampshire* struck a mine off the west coast of Orkney and sank almost immediately. Britain's military hero was not among the handful of survivors.

The turn of Errington Angus was to come a quarter of a century later, when he was Chief Steward aboard the *Aelybryn* (4,986 tons), homeward bound with a cargo of tea from Cochin in India. On 10 March 1943 she developed engine trouble and had to drop behind her convoy to carry out repairs. Late on the following day she set out to catch up with the others, but at 21.30 hrs that evening she was hit by two torpedoes.

"I jumped out of my bunk on to a floor already knee-deep in water. The Chief, from the next cabin, shouted that the boats must be smashed, and he was heading for'ard to the rafts. He was never seen again, though we looked all around for him after she went down. I went to my boat station, and mine was the only one still working; we picked up some survivors, and we ended up with thirty-two men on that lifeboat – eight, we learned later, had been killed in the explosion.

"The U-Boat surfaced alongside and called for our captain, but he huddled down out of sight, and we shouted that he'd gone down with the ship. He whispered that he wasn't going to be made a prisoner, and he'd made the right decision, for the submarine commander just wished us *bon voyage* and told us to shove off. After five days of rowing we were picked up by a Portuguese passenger ship that took us to Cape Town, and after three weeks of sunshine and South African hospitality we sailed home in style on the Queen Mary."

A. J. Vinden was born in 1890, and at the age of ninety two he is both lucid and lyrical in his memories of his days at sea. They were adventurous, and included two horrendous sinkings.

"The first came in August 1916, when I was a pantryman aboard the *Transylvania*, a big passenger ship carrying between three and four thousand troops to India. When the torpedo hit us, one boat full of Red Cross nurses was lowered away, but they had only two men in there to crew it, so I slid down a rope and picked up an oar. We pulled clear, and then we picked up men struggling in the water, but eventually we were loaded to the gunwales and couldn't take any more.

"There were still at least a thousand men aboard the *Transylvania*, with no life-boats, no hope – and would you believe it, these lads were lining the rails, singing the old army songs, as they went down with the ship. Many hours later the Italians, who were our allies at that time, sent out trawlers to pick us up, and when we went ashore we had to step over rows and rows of bodies that had been washed up. They bedded us down in the ornate grandeur of the Opera House in Genoa, and later they organised a grand parade of all the survivors, led by an Italian Army band playing Chopin's Funeral March on silver trumpets. It was very impressive, and very moving – but we had a lot to mourn as we marched. All these brave, gallant soldiers, and a lot of our shipmates, went down with the old *Transylvania*."

In the following year, on 1 December 1917, A. J. Vinden was a pantryman aboard another troopship, this time bound for Egypt, when a similar disaster occurred, and although there was again a horrendous loss of life, the moment he remembers now as particularly poignant concerned just one man, name and status unknown. "She went down very fast by the stern, the *Lansowe Castle*, and as I sat there safe in the life-boat I saw just one poor fellow, silhouetted against the sky, all alone up there on the fo'c'sle, about a hundred feet or more above the water, clinging to the rail with not one single hope ahead of him."

Clad only in his pyjamas as he made his dash for survival, Vinden had snatched an abandoned greatcoat from an empty cabin, and he had huddled warm in the life-boat as he and his shipmates waited to be picked up by their escorting Japanese destroyers – Japan, in 1917, was Britain's ally, not her enemy.

As he marched up the rescuer's gangplank A. J. Vinden became almost certainly the first ship's pantryman to piped aboard a warship of the Imperial Japanese Navy by a ceremonial guard of honour. The greatcoat he had filched in his flight, heavily laden with gold braid, belonged to the *Lansowe Castle's* Chief Officer.

The Merchant Navy's Roll of Honour stretches wide as well as long, and it includes the names of men of many nations; Indians, Lascars, Chinese, Finns, Norwegians, Portuguese and Swedes. One of the most interesting is to be found in the war memorial in Edinburgh Castle. Luigi Francesco Togneri was a doctor of medicine born and educated in Scotland, and on the outbreak of war in 1939 he at once volunteered for service in the armed forces of what he rightly regarded as his native country. Because his parents had been born Italian, however, he was informed that he could not be commissioned, although he could be accepted into the army in some menial capacity. He turned instead to the Merchant Navy, which did not observe such fine distinctions, and in September 1939 he sailed for South Georgia aboard the *New Sevilla*, as a ship's surgeon bound for duty with the Antarctic whaling fleet. This was very much a wartime mission, for the by-products of the pelagic whale include glycerine, and glycerine was vital to the manufacture of explosives.

Throughout two full whaling seasons, and two further years engaged in transatlantic convoys, Luigi Togneri kept a detailed diary of life at sea, in the form of a series of letters preserved by his widow and handed on by her to their son. They paint a dramatic picture of conditions, and of human behaviour and relationships under stress in an ocean that in 1982 has once again become familiar to British seamen under attack.

He wrote with admiration of the quiet fortitude of the typical deep-sea sailor, with mingled pride and distress about the operations he had been compelled to perform under appalling conditions, with unmitigated disgust about another young doctor who, unable to stand the strain and the danger, had turned himself first into an alcoholic and later into a hopeless drug addict by the simple expedient of systematically looting the ship's medicine store of the narcotics intended to relieve other men's pain. There was little soft however, about Togneri: Before losing his life when his ship was torpedoed in June 1944 he had taken his turn beside the harpoon gunners in the little catching boats, and he had been awarded the MBE for gallantry in action in the South Atlantic.

On 8 June 1982 the British people learned of the death of Captain Ian North, master of the container ship *Atlantic Conveyor* (14,760 tons) sunk in the

South Atlantic by air-launched Exocet missiles. The attack had come just before dawn on Argentina's National Day, May 25, and Captain North had been the last man to leave his stricken ship, scorning safety in favour of a final search for wounded survivors. He left it too late to save himself, and was last seen groping around the edges of a life raft, seconds before drowning in the icy waters of the Antarctic. His men say of him: "It was just what you would expect of him – he was a magical man, a great skipper, and we'd have done anything for him. He was tough and white-bearded – we knew him as Captain Bird's Eye – and he was talented, too. One of his ways of boosting morale was to draw a cartoon of a different member of the ship's company each day and to post it on the bridge – and they were bloody good cartoons. But above all he was fair and friendly, and he had time for every last man under his command."

The facts of that military situation are these. The British Task Force could never have sailed without the support of the Merchant Navy, the civilians who carried so many of them with their food, and their fuel to the point of action and who shared with them the hazards of the South Atlantic. When the British Government asked the National Union of Seamen whether they would offer their help, the response was spectacular. The considered estimate of Maritime House, dated 16 June 1982, is that of some five thousand seamen asked to venture into the Combat Zone, entirely of their own volition, roughly 99.9 per cent said 'yes', a fair few of them lost their lives for their fidelity, and the Falkland Islands remained British Sovereign Territory.

Chapter 29

EPILOGUE: MURMANSK, ARCHANGEL, APRIL 1982

In Murmansk and Archangel today the men of the British Merchant Navy at war are remembered with gratitude, with reverence, and with pride. They are remembered by those, both men and women, who fought and suffered by their side, by the seamen, the dockers, the longshoremen and the winch-drivers who shared with them the hardships and the dangers, the shock of the torpedoes and the horrors of aerial bombardment throughout those terrible years, four decades past, of the time of the arctic convoys.

In these two cities, the war memorials and the graves of the dead are not forgotten monuments to be hurried past or ignored. Men and women will stand bare-headed in the snow to pay tribute, and high among those who receive this posthumous respect are the British and Allied merchant seamen who died in bringing to Russia the food, the fuel and the equipment so desperately needed by that country's armies as, with twenty million of their people dead, they continued to fight on against the armies, air force and navy of Nazi Germany.

Throughout many conferences and private conversations in the International Seamen's Clubs of Murmansk and Archangel, one impression above all others was indelible, received and understood in every other discussion or communication experienced during the period of intensive research that the book has entailed, in Great Britain and elsewhere. Such men, regardless of nationality, are first and foremost *seamen*, and seamen are a race apart, with their own standards and sets of values that owe little to politics nor to place of origin. They are men, from captain to cabin boy, who in the very nature of things may be classed, almost by definition, as the true citizens of the world, who take oceans and continents in their stride throughout a lifetime of dangerous endeavour.

The men who recently gathered in these northern ports to tell their stories and to recall the days of wartime alliance included many whose names and whose personal bravery have long been legendary in their own country, and it is not to digress from the central theme of this book, the story of the British

Merchant Navy at war, that brief mention is made of them here. There were men like Badigin Konstantin, a wartime chief of staff, a famous Arctic explorer, and now one of Russia's best known authors on maritime matters. And Mark Shevelyov, Hero of the Soviet Union, renowned since 1929 as probably the greatest Polar pilot of all time, who led a bomber wing throughout the war, helping incidentally to provide, as he puts it, "the eyes of the fleet." Mikhail Kourbatov, now Vice-President of the Soviet Chartering Corporation, sailed as an A.B. in wartime convoys between Russia and Britain, as did Victor Zharkov and Piotr Gruzinsky. Vladimir Prokoviev too had long been familiar with British ports before becoming Chairman of the Archangel Regional Committee of the Sea and River Workers' Union. Valentin Amelyushkin is Chairman of the Northern War Veteran Council, which fact speaks for itself.

Bosun Pavlovsky, now an Honoured Citizen of Archangel, is a vast monolith of a man who might have been cast by Conrad, a natural leader who took over responsibility from his wounded Captain when their ship, the *Sibiriakov* had been sunk during an action against the German battleship *Admiral Scheer*, an act that saved a convoy from massacre.

And Maria Vaganova, now eighty-three years old and still shy of talking about herself. Yet she holds the Order of Lenin, and many other decorations as well, because of her courage when serving as a crane operator, during Murmansk's years of hell. Badly wounded, during an air raid, she nonetheless came back after eight months in hospital to carry on with her dangerous job in the docks. Her summing-up now is humbling: "Millions of brave men and women had given their lives – what else would one do? After work one night I went to my home, and there was no home to go to, nothing, not a stick. And so I went back to the docks and worked another shift – these seamen needed all the help they could get in unloading, for they too were under bombardment."

On 9 April 1982, during a very long and very rarely granted interview, Rear Admiral Ivan Dmitriyevich Papanin, twice Hero of the Soviet Union for his work in Polar research, now Head of the Maritime Research Department of the USSR Academy of Sciences, spoke of his duties during the years of the convoys, when he was personally responsible to his Government for all ocean transportation in northern waters. Now eighty-eight years old, Admiral Papanin remembered without prompting the incidents related in Chapter 23, and remembered also the name of the junior officer, Maurice Irvin, who had had the temerity to rebuke him for his tactless exhortation in relation to "faster discharge."

"Irvin – I remember him well, and I admired him. The *Empire Elgar*, wasn't it? Perhaps he would like a photograph to help him remember me." A sign to his secretary, and a painstaking inscription on a photograph that Maurice Irvin now treasures in his home in Welwyn Garden City.

Admiral Papanin good-humouredly accepted a bottle of vodka as a token of belated recognition of the six gargantuan containers he had presented forty years earlier to the crew of the *Empire Elgar*, and turned to more serious matters. "Probably I was asking the impossible – but in those days we were all being asked to perform the impossible. What we must all do now is to ensure that our children and our grandchildren never know the horror and the tragedy that we knew. Your seamen fought and died alongside our own against the most terrible scourge the world has ever known. They must not have died for nothing – we must have peace."

As a summing-up of all the hardship and self-sacrifice, that will serve well enough as an epitaph to the men of the Merchant Navy who gave their lives between 1939 and 1945 in their war under the red ensign.

INDEX OF SHIP NAMES

173

Strathaire: 37
Strathallan: 37
Suffolk: 58

T

Tacoma City: 146
Tamelayne: 93
The Medway Queen: 21
Thurso: 66
Tintern Abbey: 129
Tirpitz: 85, 87, 88
Tortelli: 39
Trevisa: 31
Troubador: 92

V

Viceroy of India: 46
Vienna: 113-115
Vimy: 39

W

White Crest: 44
Wild Swan: 66
Winchester Castle: 153-156
Windsor Castle: 104
Winona: 31

Z

Zwarte Zee: 60, 61

Dut.